# DID I EVER TELL YOU ABOUT THE TIME ...

How to develop and deliver a speech
using stories that get your message across

**Grady Jim Robinson**

McGraw-Hill

New York   San Francisco   Washington, D.C.   Auckland   Bogotá
Caracas   Lisbon   London   Madrid   Mexico City   Milan
Montreal   New Delhi   San Juan   Singapore
Sydney   Tokyo   Toronto

Library of Congress Catalog Number: 99-75907

# McGraw-Hill

*A Division of The **McGraw·Hill** Companies*

1 2 3 4 5 6 7 8 9 0 AGM / AGM 0 9 8 7 6 5 4 3 2 1 0

ISBN 0-07-134214-1

*Printed and bound by Quebecor Arcata/Martinsburg.*

This publication is designed to provide accurate and authoritative information in regard to the subject matter covered. It is sold with the understanding that the publisher is not engaged in rendering legal, accounting,
or other professional service. If legal advice or other expert assistance is
required, the services of a competent professional person should be
sought.

> *—From a declaration of principles jointly adopted by a committee*
> *of the American Bar Association and a committee of publishers.*

 This book is printed on recycled, acid-free paper
containing a minimum of 50% recycled de-inked fiber.

McGraw-Hill books are available at special quantity discounts to
use as premiums and sales promotions, or for use in corporate
training programs. For more information, please write to the
Director of Special Sales, Professional Publishing, McGraw-Hill, 2 Penn
Plaza, New York, NY 10121-2298. Or contact your local bookstore.

*For Wilma Robinson*
*Wittiest Girl*
*Alma High School*

# CONTENTS

# CONTENTS

# CONTENTS

# FOREWORD

A great story evokes the spirits of the past, and the dreams of the future. By listening to other people's stories and telling stories of our own, we change our perceptions, our understanding of our lives, and our understanding of the lives of people in the world around us.

Storytelling helps speakers to make a lasting impression on their listeners. Your name and face may be forgotten but an effective story will stay within the listener's mind forever. A story affects people to the core of their beings, to the depths of their souls. Stories shape lives and ideas and worldviews. It has been said that we understand *everything* through the context provided by story. As we move deeper into the age of electronically transmitted information, the context provided by story that helps us understand what all that information means becomes even more important.

Simply listening to a story told on audiotape changed my life forever. Twenty-five years ago I was building polyvinyl chloride (PVC) geodesic domes in New York City. I was successful in business and I was doing exceedingly well, until an oil embargo forced me into bankruptcy virtually overnight. It turns out that it was the best/worst experience of my life. Yes, I was at the place affectionately known as the pits (or, as Grady Jim is going to show you in this very book, the Supreme Ordeal). We all get to visit that place on our respective journeys through life; the great thing is that you don't have to stay there.

I was at the lowest point in my life when someone gave me an audiotape. I started listening and was wowed down to the fiber of my soul. I was upside down and had nothing else important to do, so ultimately I listened to that tape 287 times. The tape was called "Are You the Cause or Are You the Effect?" Through the power of a story, Cavett Robert changed my life. Did he know he was going to make such a profound change in my life? I doubt it. He told a story, not knowing who would listen. He was talking to me, my heart, my soul, and my very being and essence. I was listening with my ears but my mind took hold of it, and so did my soul. The message Cavett was trying to convey was that I was either the creature of circumstance or the creator. I understood what he was saying because he told it in story form. He didn't just admonish or encourage ... he told a story.

I chose to change my life because of Cavett Robert's story. I knew that I wanted to make a positive impact on people's lives, and I knew that I wanted to do that by becoming a speaker and a writer. Now I teach, preach, and practice that one person, with one story, makes a difference. The cards and letters that I receive in response to the *Chicken Soup for the Soul®* stories show that the simple act of telling a story can influence people throughout the world.

My friend Grady Jim has written an exceptional book called *Did I Ever Tell You about the Time ...* . Grady Jim is one of the speaking industry's premier storytellers and is acknowledged widely as one who understands how and why stories work. His workshops on personal storytelling fill up quickly, and speakers from around the world have been deeply influenced by his commitment to the Hero's Journey story model that he explores in this book. Many professional speakers, teachers, trainers, and preachers today, inspired by Grady Jim's pioneering work, fill their programs and sermons with personal, self-revealing stories that include a twist of pain but close with redeeming humor.

Grady Jim writes to the storyteller in everyone and teaches us how to recognize the perfect story, preferably right out of our own life experiences, that will make a lasting impression on the people who hear it.

We are forever on a journey, experiencing our respective challenges and our Supreme Ordeals in the guise of oil embargoes, downsizing, mergers, disease, or failed projects. We then find our own victories within the journey. Sometimes the victory is simply the courage to see it all with humor and to get up and try again.

Read this book, and let its stories have an impact on your life. More importantly, learn how great storytellers discover, develop over a period of time and hard work, and then deliver stories that reshape lives. Become a great storyteller, and elevate your platform power.

Mark Victor Hansen
Coauthor, *Chicken Soup for the Soul*

# ACKNOWLEDGMENTS

In the writing of this book, I discovered that it is much easier for me to tell a story than it is to write a book about how others can tell their stories.

Without the help of several very loyal colleagues and friends, this book would yet remain within my own world of fantasy.

My deepest thanks to Linda Kott of Eventing Concepts, who supported me during my year of wilderness wandering and the writing of this book; and to my agent Georgia Hughes, who found the right publisher. Thanks to Cheryl Kimbo, who untangled my computerized files. And a very special thank-you to Irena Tatkiawicz, who demonstrated optimism, faith, and good humor when my own energy weakened.

Thanks to McGraw-Hill editor Betsy Brown, who believed in this book enough to wait patiently just a bit longer; and to a talented Mari Florence, who rode in on a white horse at the last minute.

Without Deb Lilly as the hub of this circle of feminine power, I would still be contemplating what to do next.

And finally, a loving thank you to Jane Seagraves of St. Louis, my ten-year associate, dear friend, and loyal support system, who views every supreme ordeal in my life—and not just the literary ones—as just a bit of a challenge.

# INTRODUCTION

I have used stories to entertain and teach for 25 years. The magic of storytelling first became apparent to me in the sermons and classes I led during my ten years as a minister. Later I called upon stories in a much different role as a stand-up comedian. Eventually, by applying what I had learned from both realms, I used story power as a professional speaker.

It became immediately clear to me during my earliest days as a young sermonizer that a story instantly captured the listeners. Whether it was a classic biblical tale such as "David and Goliath" or a personal story about growing up in Arkansas, the listeners were riveted from beginning to end.

In this book we will explore why stories possess a mysterious power to mesmerize audiences both large and small. I will show you how your childhood stories, when constructed, developed, and delivered in the proper way, resonate at the deepest level in every listener and have a transforming effect similar to that of ancient myth, classic literature, and modern cinematography. Whether you are a professional speaker, a corporate trainer, a minister, a lawyer, or a teacher, you can dramatically increase audience impact through story power.

In 1979 I published my first story in *Sports Illustrated.* During the next ten years, 26 others appeared in that publication and dozens of other magazines or newspapers. During that time, I was pursuing multiple careers as a freelance writer, motivational humorist, and stand-up comedian—anything to keep from getting a real job until I could become the next Great American Novelist. The stories that first appeared in print were developed later in front of live audiences (well, most of them were live) at comedy clubs and convention banquets.

Many of those early stories were about growing up in Arkansas as the second son of the high school football coach. I was totally unaware that my childhood stories, most of which revolved around my attempts to win the approval of my father, had serious psychological and archetypal implications.

In 1987, along with millions of other baby boomers, I discovered Joseph Campbell through his PBS interviews with Bill Moyers. These interviews were later published as *The Power of Myth,* which eventually hit *The New York Times* bestseller list. While listening to Campbell speak with charm and passion about the role of myth in our lives, it slowly dawned on me that my stories about growing up in Arkansas were very similar to myths, legends, and folk tales from around the world. My interest led me to other mythologists such as Otto Rank and Mircea Eliade, psychologist Carl Jung, writer James Joyce, and further to the use of myth by major filmmakers such as George Lucas and Steven Spielberg.

Your childhood stories are just as profound and powerful as any classic tale ever told. Your fishing trip with grandpa, your first bike ride, that rite-of-passage experience with your father or mother that changed your life—all are minimyths that contain the same psychological, emotional, moral, and spiritual life-shaping potential as *The Odyssey* or *Star Wars*.

I have separated this book into three parts. Part I is devoted to an exploration of the story type known as the Hero's Journey—that universal experience of human struggle and triumph found in everything from myths and fairy tales to plays, novels, and movies. Hero's Journey or Hero's Quest tales and myths are common to all cultures. Because they generally have three distinct phases, they are readily identified and understood by readers or listeners and are relatively easy to develop into high-impact stories. We will study the three phases that Campbell referred to as separation, initiation, and integration and that I call:

- Take the Journey
- Face the Challenge
- Find the Victory

I want you to have complete confidence in the necessity of three phases—not just two—and to understand why phase II of the journey is most important.

Part II shifts to the more practical aspects of storytelling—specifically, discovery and development. Where do stories originate? Is it fair to make up stories for speeches? Why are childhood stories so effective? And what about the use of exaggeration? We will also explore the role of humor in Hero's Journey stories. We will see clearly that humor generally results when the hero is defeated or when the journey has gone awry. How do we find humor in defeat? Stories developed for public speaking are most effective when they contain humor. And, surprisingly, we will see that the most important aspect in creating humor is the context.

In Part III, we finally arrive at the fun part (and the difficult part): making the speech. Delivery of the story in front of a live audience is a daring act. This mysterious form of communication that I call Relationship Style speaking is the direct descendent of what was known as Participatory Style—acting and oratory in the pre–Civil War period of American history. (This style emphasized a connection between speaker and audience.) You will learn to share your own journey. We will explore the use of voice, intonation, rhythm, body language, facial expressions, and other aspects of delivery, moving beyond mechanical skill into the realm of unexplained domains such as passion and authenticity that ultimately define success.

## SYNOPSES OF HERO'S JOURNEY STORIES

We'll be looking at six stories throughout this book that serve as clear examples of the Hero's Journey. Two are modern films, one is a Pulitzer Prize–winning novel (and a TV miniseries), two are my own short stories ("Facing Fishook" and "Pine Tar"), and the last is the ancient epic *Beowulf.* Here are brief synopses of these stories. As you peruse these versions of the stories that are bared to the bone, you may be able to see certain phases in each one. A one-two-three process may appear.

1. *Star Wars*

   Luke Skywalker is the son of a Jedi fighter who was killed in action. The Dark Side led by Darth Vader threatens once again. Luke is called by Obie Wan Kenobie to join other Jedi fighters to battle the Dark Side. Luke is reluctant to answer the call. But, armed with the Force and the secrets of Obie Wan Kenobie, he enters the fray.

   Many challenges arise. Ships fail, Princess Leia is taken captive, and so on. We approach the supreme ordeal—the Star Fleet battle where Luke is down to his last rocket. Just as he engages the radar, a voice says, "Use the Force, Luke."

   He fires. Bull's-eye. The victory is won and he returns home the hero.

2. *Apollo 13*

   Captain Jim Lovell and crew blast off, leaving the everyday world for the uncertainties of outer space. Challenge after challenge is faced and met through ingenuity, teamwork, science, and precision planning. A makeshift guidance system fires the ship toward home. Survival seems impossible as they approach the supreme ordeal of re-entry.

A blackout occurs as all await the fate of the ship and crew.

They emerge victorious, returning to Earth as conquering heroes.

3. *Lonesome Dove*

Colonel Woodrow Call and Augustus McCrae come out of retirement, round up a herd of cattle, gather a crew of young, inexperienced cowboys, and head north to the promised land of Montana. They face raging rivers, snakes, evil personified in Blue Duck the renegade killer, bad luck, Indians, and more.

Cohero Gus McRae is wounded and, rather than have both legs amputated, takes his own life. Col. Call takes the body back to Lonesome Dove for burial, initiating yet another Hero's Journey with seemingly endless challenges of its own.

4. "Facing Fishook"

Our Little League hero is reluctant to answer the call in this rite-of-passage experience. Fishook is an imposing pitcher for the opposing team. When the time arrives to face Fishook, the hero refuses the call by hiding in the ballfield outhouse. His father bangs on the door and threatens to knock it down if the little hero does not come out.

He emerges and walks toward home plate, where he is given the secret key by the coach-father, who says, "The ball will curve. Don't duck."

The boy stands ready for the supreme ordeal. Fishook throws the ball and the boy refuses to duck. But alas, he's been given bad instructions, and the hero is beaned in the head by a fastball. You will find the entire story in Chapter 8.

5. "Pine Tar"

   In this personal story, my father forces me to play in my first basketball game, unaware that I am afraid to wear shorts in public. I walk onto the floor, where an embarrassing scene occurs. The next day I try out for the team and eventually star in high school and college basketball. (This story is found in Chapter 12.)

6. *Beowulf*

   Beowulf travels to the land of Wrothgar to battle the spirit-monster Grendel. He will fight for the King, who has been threatened by evil Grendel for 12 years. Beowulf is given a special sword.

   The battle takes place and Beowulf, most eager for fame, defeats Grendel. There is a big celebration, but while the men sleep off their victory party a more ominous and powerful monster stealthily appears at the door: Grendel's mother. She kills and consumes many of the King's finest warriors.

   Beowulf follows in pursuit, descending into the underwater world of the spirit-monster, where a magnificent battle ensues. Beowulf is actually on his back with the monster at his throat when he sees a famous sword on the wall. He reaches for it and cuts off the monster's head.

   He returns to his own land, where he rules as a good and just king for 50 years.

We will explore these stories and others in the following pages. Each of these six stories contains within it three clear phases: (I) The hero undertakes separation or movement toward a goal or prize, (II) immediate obstacles and challenges occur that make up the main body, (III) a conclusion or wrap-up of some kind completes the story.

As you think about story formation, it will be helpful to imagine the circle of movement I call the Hero's Journey.

# The Hero's Journey

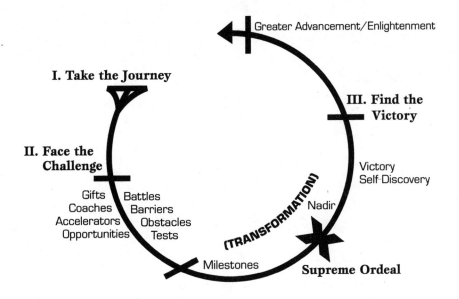

Greater Advancement/Enlightenment

I. Take the Journey

III. Find the Victory

II. Face the Challenge

Victory
Self-Discovery

Gifts    Battles
Coaches    Barriers
Accelerators    Obstacles
Opportunities    Tests

(TRANSFORMATION)

Nadir

Milestones    Supreme Ordeal

# THE POWER OF THE HERO'S JOURNEY

# 1 THE DAY I BECAME THE STORY

I was surprisingly calm, standing behind the curtain straightening my tie as I was being introduced to the Million Dollar Round Table's opening session in San Francisco. MDRT, as it is known in the meetings industry, is widely recognized as the Super Bowl (or the Academy Awards, if you don't like sports metaphors) of professional speaking.

Facing more than 4,000 successful insurance salespersons is daunting. But there I stood, about to speak to one of the most demanding audiences in the world, eager to grab the microphone, look them in the eye, and say, "My Daddy was a football coach in Arkansas … ."

Just before I rode onto the stage in a miniature cable car, a strange feeling came over me. There was an instant flashback over the previous 25 years of public speaking. Dancing through my mind were various images: a tall, very young, minister standing in front of a hundred high school kids around a campfire; a young man speaking from a flatbed truck at a county fair; a storyteller from Arkansas yelling into a microphone at Catch a Rising Star, the legendary comedy club in New York City; and dozens more. As I prepared to ride out on stage I thought about an audience I had faced years earlier: six hundred squirming seventh graders corralled for the compulsory daily chapel service.

At the time, I was a young minister and often had the opportunity to address youth groups. I had already become a fairly accomplished speaker, but this unruly mass of preteenagers posed the ultimate challenge.

I watched and listened as they scrambled to find their seats in the Harding Academy auditorium in Memphis, Tennessee. They had become accustomed to the continuous parade of preachers in dark suits, warning them in the typically solemn, rich tones of the Southern evangelist about the dangers of dancing, short skirts, drinking, and other temptations.

During the first hymn I pondered my "sermon" notes. Then suddenly I heard a voice from somewhere deep within say, "Just tell them a good story!"

I'd like to think that voice was deep instinctual wisdom. But I was only 23 at the time, so it was probably sheer luck (and panic).

Thank God, I listened to that inner voice. My decision to follow story power would prove to be a crucial turning point in my life. At a very early age for a professional speaker, teacher, or communicator, I was about to discover, quite by accident, what I call the "trance"-forming power of story—the incredible and seemingly mysterious capacity of stories to mesmerize any audience, from seventh-grade assemblies to the Million Dollar Round Table.

I confess that it would be almost two decades before I understood how and why stories work. On this day, through the well-known biblical tale of "David and Goliath," I was simply thrilled to witness and experience this mysterious power in story. When I walked onto the podium and immediately launched into this epic story, I had no clue that David and Goliath were well-known mythical archetypes. Nor did I know that those characters were deeply ingrained in the collective unconscious of all those seventh graders and every audience I would ever face. David was and remains a universal symbol of the hero and Goliath a universal symbol of the great foe, the enemy, the monster.

Most of the stories I would create and tell over the next 20 years would place me in the role of hero, or better stated, the frustrated hero, which is the origin of humor. Goliath is another classic archetype, the foe, the obstacle. The symbol of the foe would also appear in my stories as my own father, as Fishook, and even as a big snake.

We will look more carefully at this important idea of universal archetype in stories in a later chapter.

What I discovered that day is that there's mystery and magic in a story. Yes, a story must contain certain elements to be effective. But the way you tell the story is of equal importance. Standing before 600 wide-eyed seventh graders, I did not read the story, nor did I simply tell the story—I *became* the story.

In the first-person voice of young David (the hero), I told the listeners how I had been sent into a war zone by my father to take provisions to my older brothers. Then, in the roaring voice of Goliath, I issued a challenge to the Hebrew army to send a single brave soldier onto the battlefield.

Within seconds the auditorium fell deathly quiet. Eyes wide, mouths agape, those little faces were glued to me in anticipation of 14-year-old David, armed only with a slingshot, facing the huge, hairy giant who was wearing metal armor with a shield and waving an immense sword. Naturally, I embellished just a bit, or let's just say modernized the tale by comparing Goliath to Hulk Hogan and David to a teen pop star at the time, Shaun Cassidy. The battle itself, I assured them, was being broadcast on pay-per-view cable where the winner would be crowned World Champion and get a huge movie deal. The kids loved it. Certain teachers were not amused.

Acting out the role of David, I bent down into the river bed and chose five stones. I placed one in my imaginary slingshot, which I explained was "usually made with tennis shoe strings and the tongue of an old leather shoe." Whirling it about my head, I hissed and made a loud swishing sound into the microphone: "Sssshhhoop-sssshhhoop-sssshhhooop!" The audience gasped as the stone flew like a bullet toward Goliath and then, wham-o, smacked the giant right between the eyes.

Playing out my double role, I crashed to the floor, bringing the microphone stand down with a loud clang. (Being six feet, five inches tall must have added a certain authenticity to the scene.) They stood and cheered as young David (me again) approached the fallen giant, took his huge sword and, in a dramatic ending—swissshhh—cut off the giant's head. A bit violent, I suppose, but that's the story.

Then I sat down. I uttered no admonitions, no exhortations, no thou shalt not's, no commentary whatever. The story spoke for itself with a thousand different messages. Among those 600 tender souls that day were literally dozens of unique life-shaping situations to which the classic story could be applied. A young boy facing fears of a giant enemy, a young girl dealing with sibling issues at home, other children feeling weak or less than capable of dealing with the Great Foes in their own lives.

The story spoke to those situations and many more.

The next day, as I sat in my office pondering my ministerial duties, I received a phone call from Dr. Harold Bowie, superintendent of Harding Academy. "James," he said as I held my breath, "those kids just loved your talk yesterday. I don't know what you did, but you must come back every week."

I dared to breathe and said, "I'd love to."

"We can pay you $25 a week."

Over the next four years I spoke every Thursday at the chapel service. Within a few months I began to experiment with all kinds of stories and realized that the most effective ones were based on my own personal experiences as an adolescent and teenager, usually those dealing with my father the coach and my attempts to play sports.

During the next two decades my life became a journey to discover, develop, and deliver my own stories. It eventually also became my livelihood.

The miniature cable car suddenly whisked me onto the stage and into the spotlight, the spotlight of professional speaking. That day I told stories: the story of my football coach father, the story of my own son playing Little League baseball, and the story about me being in the Canary reading group in the second grade. How can a personal story contain universal truths? How does a story about a boy growing up in Arkansas as the second son of the football coach resonate with, for example, an African-American woman who grew up in Harlem?

Through the magic and mystery of story as symbol, human beings share in common life's most meaningful rite-of-passage experiences.

At the end of the 25-minute program, I received a standing ovation. Any success I've had as a speaker-humorist-storyteller is not the result of my talent or platform skills. It is due to the transforming, mysterious power of storytelling that I instinctively pursued 25 years ago.

While the force behind storytelling may seem mysterious, there are certain components we can understand and explore. With the help of pioneers in psychology and mythology, I uncovered a process through my own personal journey of storytelling and speaking. It's this process that we will explore in this book. Through proper construction of your stories, you too can enjoy the satisfaction of captivating any audience.

## NOTES

My first audiences were young people. We had loads of fun and I enjoyed telling and reliving many life experiences on stage. Later I developed stories about growing up in Arkansas as the second son of the football coach in front of adult audiences. Young people and adults react very differently to stories. We'll explore this phenomenon as we move along in this study.

My early attempts at humor were mostly ad lib and spontaneous. Even though I was the class clown in high school, I had no experience in the creation of dependable comedy material. My early speeches were amusing and filled with enthusiasm but lacking in solid humor. In 1980 I walked into a comedy club, Bilbo Baggins' Back Room in St. Louis, and signed up for open mike night. It was there I began to develop humor and eventually became a headliner. Humor is serious business. I often encourage new speakers to visit comedy clubs and become regulars at open mike night. Very few have the courage to try it, but those who do eventually develop high-quality comedy material. The humor we will discuss in Part III is grounded in solid principles and hard work. You can learn to be funny, but it will require effort.

# 2 THE TRANCE-FORMING POWER OF STORY

I was sitting at a round table near the stage in the banquet room of the Hyatt Hotel in Dallas, entering my "zone"—that state of concentrated energy and anticipation that a speaker should enter just before the introduction. Suddenly the meeting planner leaned toward me and whispered. "Relax, Grady Jim, you're not on yet. I've got a little surprise for the troops."

I don't like surprises just before my introduction.

The 500 salesmen were restless and demanding more wine. I'm convinced the toughest audience in the world is an all-male audience after dinner and drinks. Before I could inquire about the nature of the surprise, there was a sudden explosion of sound and onto the stage burst a tidal wave of blond hair, long legs, teeth, and pompons like a Picasso suddenly coming to life and jumping off the canvas. It was the Dallas Cowboy Cheerleaders, prancing, dancing, and gyrating to the beat of a megadecibel sound system.

They strutted (danced?), contorted, and whipped their hips wildly while flashing all those white teeth through all that blond hair and, naturally, whipped the troops into a frenzy.

Now, I do like football. I even like the Cowboys. And I appreciate the dedication, hard work, and commitment of these fine young aerobics artists—but please, not before I speak!

During the 25-minute program, I carefully watched the audience and reorganized my opening remarks in my mind. The men behaved in the fashion you might expect in response to such a program: hoots and howls and a variety of the immature yelps we normally associate with teenagers at a Ricky Martin concert. Finally, the dedicated dancers exited the stage. The meeting planner then jumped to the platform amidst the uproar and, as the mob chanted, "We want more!" yelled into the microphone: "And now, our speaker for the evening."

I walked to the platform while the audience continued to shout, throw napkins in the air, and slap high-fives. The room was a madhouse. I pulled the microphone out of the holder and stared at all these husbands, grandfathers, fathers, and sons who were behaving like a lust-filled horde. I did not speak for several seconds.

Is it possible to make a speech after such a program? What means, method, technique, trick of the trade, or power from on high can a speaker call upon to capture the attention of such an audience?

Let the record show that within approximately 40 seconds, every one of those men was totally and eerily silent, transformed, transfixed, and listening in a trancelike state to a story.

I attribute the miraculous transformation of the audience not to my skill as a storyteller, but to the mystical, psychological power of story—quite possibly the most important art form available for the shaping of human lives.

## THE POWER OF STORY AS SYMBOL

The story with which I chose to open on that occasion was about my mother, who worked her way through college by washing dishes in the school cafeteria. As I walked slowly across the stage, the room began to settle down. I allowed them to look at me and fix their gaze upon the speaker. Through my body language, I displayed a certain amount of disdain for the audience, a subtle but obvious reproach for their sexist behavior. It was a challenging stance, and risky, but I knew that I had the moral high ground for an unspoken challenge.

At precisely the right second, I began to speak in a low but very clear voice, careful to use a rhythmic pattern that provided an auditory fixation point: "She was tall, gorgeous … her dream was to be a schoolteacher, but she didn't have one single dollar to go to college. (pause) Her father died when she was 2. So she washed dishes in the school cafeteria (pause) twice a day, every day, and earned her way through Center Baptist College to become a schoolteacher. She was my mother."

The audience was immediately engaged, fixed, and entranced by the story. This particular story was in stark contrast to the entertainment presented mere seconds earlier, a slight shock to their emotional system. They were seized, challenged, mystified and shocked by the dramatic shift in thoughts, images, and symbols and forced to reexamine their behavior and feelings of the past 25 minutes. As their minds shifted from scantily clad dancers to a lone woman working her way through a Baptist college, there was an immediate transformation in their minds from sex-goddess archetype to mother archetype. Then they subconsciously connected with their own mothers, sisters, and daughters. Each man then entered into an instant search process and accepted the fact that the women they had just viewed as sex objects were symbolically their own daughters or mothers—thus, the tomblike silence. I then moved immediately into humor, allowing comic relief.

Was I aware of the role of feminine archetypes? Did I purposely use the methods of Milton Erickson to fixate the audience on my body language, and shock with story so that I might "explore the listener's world and facilitate rapport and therefore create new frames of reference and belief systems"?

Well, the answer is yes and no.

As a veteran speaker, I knew instinctively how to deal with that audience. But I confess it was many months before I began to understand exactly the *what, why,* and *how* of what had occurred in the minds of the listeners.

## THE STORYTELLER AS TRANCE-TELLER

In her book, *Women Who Run with Wolves,* author, analyst, and self-proclaimed *cantadora* Clarissa Pinkola Estes, Ph.D., writes, "Story is far older than the art and science of psychology, and will always be the elder in the equation no matter how much time passes. One of the oldest ways of telling, which intrigues me greatly, is the passionate trance state, wherein the teller 'senses' the audience—be it an audience of one or of many—and then enters a state in the world between worlds, where a story is 'attracted' to the trance-teller and told through her. This is the storyteller furthering soul-making."

### What Do We Mean by Trance-Teller?

Milton Erickson pioneered the use of hypnotherapy as an accepted method for the treatment of mental patients.

Thanks to the work of Erickson, millions of former smokers have kicked the habit through hypnotherapy. Sports professionals from golfers to football players have achieved peak performance through hypnotherapy techniques developed by Erickson and his associates.

The part of Erickson's research that is of most importance to the speaker is the technique he developed in putting his patient into the trance state necessary for hypnotherapy. Instead of relying on the classic means of trance inducement, such as a candle or dangling watch as a fixation point, Erickson discovered that the telling of a story was a much better method. The parallels between the speaker–listener relationship and the therapist–patient relationship in the work of Erickson provide us with a rich vein of resources for deeper understanding of the potential power of story.

## THE STORY AS TRANCE-FORMING POINT

As a speaker who long ago discovered the mesmerizing and spellbinding power of storytelling, I am struck by the parallels between Erickson's use of storytelling in hypnotherapy and the speaker's use of storytelling on the platform. We speakers learned way back in the caveperson days (this was, of course, after the discovery of fire, which was immediately followed by fried chicken and the inevitable banquet) that audiences are quickly engaged by a story. We must admit, however, that we didn't know exactly how or why.

In *Hypnotherapy: An Exploratory Casebook* by Milton Erickson and Dr. Ernest Rossi, we learn how and why listeners routinely enter a trancelike state when listening to a story.

Let's define what we mean exactly by the word *trance*. The trance state in hypnotherapy is *not* the cartooned conception made popular by our old friend Wile E. Coyote. Remember those concentric circles going round and round in his glazed eyes? Please! According to Erickson, "trance is a natural state that each of us fall into and out of many times during a normal day." Sidney Rosen, in his book about the storytelling techniques of Erickson, *My Voice Will Go with You,* writes, "Trance, in fact, is a natural state experienced by everyone. Our most familiar trance experience takes place when we daydream, pray, meditate or even jog." Trance is not necessarily the deep, sleeplike hypnotic trance that we mistakenly associate with the word itself. By scientific definition it is simply a period of concentration when "a person is aware of the vividness of inner mental and sensory experiences, and therefore *external* stimuli, such as sounds and movements assume lesser importance."

Speakers experience listeners who are entranced or spellbound in almost every speech. The deeply attentive and singularly focused listener can be said to be literally entranced: focused on the inner mental experience of thought brought about by the speaker and therefore somewhat unaware of movements around him or her, the passage of time, or what might otherwise be disturbing sounds in an adjoining room.

## FIVE STAGES OF TRANCE-FORMATION

Our interest as speakers in the work of Erickson is twofold: first, his method of trance inducement through story, and, second, the three phases of the therapeutic process. Let's look at the five stages of trance induction as described in *Hypnotherapy.* We can make some applications to similar stages in our audiences.

## Stage One: Fixation of Attention

The classical approach to fixation of attention in hypnotherapy was the therapist asking a patient to gaze upon a watch or candle flame. Later, hypnotherapists learned that it was more effective to focus the patient's attention on his or her own "inner experience." Erickson took this idea a step further and simply invited the patient to fix upon a "current experience." Erickson did this by telling a story that initially seemed not to relate to the patient and caused the patient some confusion, surprise, and wonder. And in that state of mystification and contemplation, the therapist and patient shared and were fixed upon this current experience. In reality, the story itself, perhaps unrelated to the patient's problem, connected the therapist and patient in a unique, never-before-experienced moment for *both* of them, creating this current experience (the fixation point and thus a slight trance state) where the patient is totally focused on the present moment. The patient is in trance, transfixed on the moment.

Speakers connect with listeners in exactly the same way. As the speaker begins to speak, they are in a shared current experience of auditory and visual fixation. A speaker can begin that important moment of fixation and trance by saying something like, "Thank you for that fine introduction." Or, "It's good to be with you here in Topeka." These statements connect speaker and audience in a current experience moment. However, as we will see later, a story, with all its potential imagery and symbol, is a much more potent shared current experience for both the speaker and the audience. Interestingly enough, the most powerful means of bringing about current experience is with the use of humor. Erickson discovered that a pun or a joke or a funny story was more powerful than a story without sizzle.

## Stage Two: Breaking Away to New Awareness

The speaker's purpose is to move the audience to new and better ways of thinking, feeling, being, or perceiving. The listener cannot or will not move to new ways of thinking until he or she is willing to reexamine and possibly move out of old ways of thinking, being, and so on. The first task of the speaker, then, is to invite the audience to reexamine habitual forms of thinking. How is this accomplished? In the therapist–patient relationship, this stage was termed by Rossi and Erickson as "depotentiating habitual frameworks and belief systems."

Erickson discovered that patients, when slightly mystified or shocked by his seemingly unrelated story or delighted by his humor, opened their minds for a brief moment to new ways of thinking. Wondering what the therapist was saying, they were forced to search their minds for a brief moment for new ways of seeing things. "What is he saying to me?" "Am I stupid for not understanding?" "What am I missing here?" These questions send the subconscious mind on a frantic search for a way of grasping what is being said. Rossi described this as the "creative moment."

"A creative moment occurs when a habitual pattern of association is interrupted," according to Rossi. It is a gap in one's normal way of seeing things, and the thought or light that fills that gap is the genius of original thinking. It is not unlike what occurs when your teenage son accidentally throws a football against the window blinds. The impact of the ball forces the individual blinds to separate for an instant, new light enters the room, and then the blinds automatically fall back into place.

In everyday life, we are constantly confronted with mystifying and mildly shocking information or situations that defy our usual ways of thinking. In those moments one is forced to think new thoughts. And in order to think new thoughts, one must challenge and sometimes discard old ways of thinking.

When a speaker tells a story, a listener is instantly exposed to symbols and images that invite one to rethink old information and habitually accepted ways of feeling, seeing, perceiving, and being.

A listener is invited, but not forced, into potentially different ways of seeing things.

## Stage Three: Unconscious Search

The third state in actuality is what we have already mentioned in stage two. (It's impossible to describe the breaking-away process without introducing the unconscious search process because the whole cannot literally be broken into distinctly separate stages; the process occurs almost instantly and simultaneously.) The instant a listener is intrigued, shocked by a bit of humor, or mystified by a strange story, the listener is opened to a creative moment and an unconscious search begins—which leads to stage four.

## Stage Four: Unconscious Process

Erickson called the entire process of fixation, trance, breaking away of old forms of thought, searching for new ways of seeing and thinking (the creative moment) "the unconscious process."

## Stage Five: Hypnotic Response

"The hypnotic response," according to Rossi, "is the *natural outcome of the unconscious search* and processes initiated by the therapist"—or, we might add, the speaker. What will the listener do with this new awareness? It's strictly up to the listener. Lest we be accused of advocating manipulation or control of belief systems through some kind of subconscious process, let me define briefly what Erickson meant by "hypnotic response." He was aware of the misconception that hypnotherapy is a means of manipulation of other people. He attempted to correct this erroneous idea. In 1948 he wrote, "Contrary to such misconceptions the hypnotized person remains the same person. Only his behavior is altered ... behavior from his own life experience and not that of the therapist. Hypnosis does not change the person, nor does it alter his past experiential life. *It serves to permit him to learn more about himself and to express himself more adequately.*"

As I stepped onto the stage that night in Dallas, I was not fully aware of just how or why my story would instantly kick off a series of mental processes whereby the listeners were invited into new ways of thinking and being. At that time, I was an experienced storyteller who on many occasions had relied on the power of story to connect with a tough audience.

A storyteller does not have to know exactly why a story works in order for it to work, just as a golfer does not necessarily have to know how a golf swing works to be a good golfer. However, if you want to be a real pro and master the art, you must not only know *what* works, but *why* and *how* it does.

# 3 WHEN THE STUDENT IS READY

For ten years I continued to use stories both in public speaking as a motivational speaker and in my act in comedy clubs. It was obvious that they worked well, first to entertain, and at a deeper level where I could only guess how and why they worked.

I had learned from Erickson that audiences were in a state of trance when they listened to a story. It did not require clinical or scientific evidence to see that throngs of people from a wide array of backgrounds, from restless seventh graders to even more restless MCI salespeople, were enthralled and literally mesmerized through the use of stories. From scene to scene the listener is carried along, wondering what will happen next, patiently waiting for the outcome of the adventure to be revealed. It was as if I had pushed a button and their minds and focus were suspended in time and space, totally absorbed in whatever scene came next in the sequence of events. Is it possible that human beings have a common interest or a kind of built-in programming that links them to a sequential movement toward a goal?

Conversations about my speeches led me to believe that something rich and deep was happening to the listeners in at least three realms.

1. Listeners are mesmerized or entranced by the unfolding story. They suspend their primary outside concerns, worries, and preoccupations with life and volunteer to focus totally upon the unfolding story.

2. Listeners are entertained through humor. The stories I developed in comedy clubs were constructed for humor. Why they were funny was not a concern at the time. It was obvious that I was the butt of the jokes, but just how humor originates in the foiled or failed attempt of the hero to gain higher status remained a mystery.

3. Listeners are touched at the deepest level of being through something just on the edge of unknowing, something that often evoked tears, deep rumination, and self-examination within the listener as the story unfolded.

Conversations after various programs revealed that men were thinking about their relationships with their fathers or their sons. Others were deeply moved by stories of heroes who failed to attain the prize, but who got up and tried again. Parents quite often whispered to me that they would immediately shift their parenting style toward one or more of their children.

On one occasion after a fun-filled and rather challenging speech to school administrators, an African-American woman who had grown up in Harlem approached me with tears on her cheeks and said, "Those stories about your father really touched my heart."

I said, "Thank you, but I wonder how? We're from such different worlds!"

We sat down and talked about the stories and how they seemed to transcend region, race, gender, age, socioeconomic issues, and religion.

After that conversation, I knew I was onto something important.

As my reputation and exposure in the speaking industry grew, I was often chided by some of my speaking colleagues about "all that pathos" in the stories. Many people thought it was a great idea to introduce a deeper dimension into public speaking through honest self-revelation couched in top-quality humor, but others did not. I knew that it was unusual to combine pain and pathos with humor. But it was exactly where my own journey as a human being was leading me. Through therapy, I had been made aware of some life-shaping issues that I was just beginning to deal with at that point in my life. I dealt with my own pain with humor and that was beginning to emerge out of my stories.

I was determined to understand just what was happening to a listener when I told the funny story about trying to win my father's approval through sports. What deep well of emotion was triggered in an adult businesswoman when I told the story of being placed in the Canary reading group in the second grade? Why were people universally moved to tears when I shared that life-shaping moment when my mother said, "Hon, you don't have to play football for your father's love. Just be what God has given you to be." While relating those words of my mother's I have seen businessmen and -women visibly melt into themselves while seated in their chairs. Why? Is it possible that through the power of my story, using both humor and pathos, they have been slowly led into a region of total self-acceptance for the first time in their lives? Is it possible that through those life-shaping words of my mother they are hearing their mothers for the very first time?

But how could that be possible? How can that happen through a personal story?

I wanted to know and was determined to find the answer. I found that in my case the old axiom held true: When the student is ready, the teacher will appear.

My flight arrived late in Denver, so I missed the connection to St. Louis and shuttled to a hotel. Tired and frustrated, I turned on the TV and began channel surfing. Click-click-click. Suddenly there appeared on the screen a handsome gentleman chatting with Bill Moyers, the TV journalist. Their conversation was about mythology. I was interested and hung in for a moment before I would settle on Monday Night football. The gentleman was mesmerizing and he talked with passion about how mythology may hold the answers to life's deepest questions. He spoke of great myths that he referred to as Hero's Quest stories. He was so intriguing that I forgot all about the Monday Night Football game.

It was my first glimpse of the legendary scholar and philosopher Joseph Campbell. He had been teaching at Sarah Lawrence College for 40 years and had earned guru status in many circles for his work in mythology. Campbell had written dozens of books on the subject, the most popular being *The Hero with a Thousand Faces,* first published in 1949.

The PBS interview, six hours in all, struck a chord with the viewing public, and millions of baby boomers were introduced to Campbell and his passion for mythology. From this series, phrases such as the "Hero's Journey" and "Follow Your Bliss" became ingrained in our cultural consciousness.

As I listened to Moyers question Campbell about the role of myth in our lives, I experienced a series of insights that totally captured my imagination. Instantly drawn to the conversation about myth and life's meaning, I heard an inner voice say, "This is it! This is how my stories work with audiences!" The dialogue immediately revealed a connection to that instinctive decision years earlier to "just tell them a story."

The night I discovered Campbell I could hardly sleep. His concept of the Hero's Journey or Hero's Quest stories had struck a chord deep within my soul. Somehow I had immediately understood the basic idea. There is a myth or story type that is universal, and is found in virtually every culture around the world—a big story (macro-myth) that resonates with the individual story (micro-myth) within every listener due to a structure that is globally understood.

I knew that my stories captivated listeners, but it was that night while watching Campbell that I first began to see that my childhood stories were connecting with audiences on a mythological and psychological level.

As Campbell writes, "It would not be too much to say that myth is the secret opening through which the inexhaustible energies of the cosmos pour into human cultural manifestation." In his poetic, sometimes flowery style, Campbell hints that myth is the doorway to a deeper truth—beyond reason or mere facts. Science can teach us the empirical truths and laws of the universe, but it is another domain that reveals the meaning behind those laws.

Through the symbols and archetypes of story or myth, human beings connect at the deepest levels. Storytelling—like painting, music, literature, poetry, or dance—is an art form. And art in its purest state brings the viewer or listener into the very presence of the divine.

How can a speaker, using his or her own personal childhood stories, possibly provide an opening "through which the inexhaustible energies of the cosmos pour"? I believe the answer to that question is, to put it simply, the Hero's Journey. But what is this epic quest common to all cultures?

## THE HERO'S JOURNEY

Campbell's memorable description of the Hero's Journey goes like this: "A Hero ventures forth from the world of common day into a region of supernatural wonder; fabulous forces are there encountered and a decisive victory is won; the hero comes back from this mysterious adventure with the power to bestow boons on his fellow man."

The three phases are clear to see:

1. The Hero ventures forth;
2. Fabulous forces are encountered there, and a victory is won; and
3. The hero returns.

This three-phase model is at the core of a rite of passage that Campbell describes in three simple words as separation-initiation-integration. Upon first reading those three words, I heard a faint echo of recognition in my subconscious mind. At first I was puzzled and assumed the echo was just another instance of my hearing things. Then one day it hit me. Erickson! Separation-initiation-integration is another way of describing Ericksonian therapy:

1. Breaking away from habitual ways of thinking (separation);
2. Search and process of new ways of thinking, being, perceiving (initiation); and
3. Integration of the new way (integration).

Therapy is parallel to a rite-of-passage experience. The Hero's Journey story is an artistic or symbolic account of the universally shared three phases of every human passage. Joseph Campbell did not discover the underlying rite-of-passage theme in Hero's Quest stories. According to Robert

Torrance, professor of Comparative Literature at the University of California at Davis, a European anthropologist named Van Gennep first coined a similar trio—separation, transition, incorporation—in his 1908 publication, *The Rites of Passage.*

Campbell referred to the phases or stages as:

1.  The Call;

2.  Threshold Crossing; and

3.  Return.

In my own workshops, I've edited the wording somewhat for immediate clarification:

1.  Take the Journey;

2.  Face the Challenge; and

3.  Find the Victory.

It is this simplistic language that will guide you to the profound heart of your stories. Each story or anecdote should include these three basic steps.

*Star Wars* is the most obvious modern example of a mythological Hero's Journey. (Director George Lucas acknowledges his debt to the Hero's Journey mode of story-telling; in fact, the Moyers–Campbell PBS interviews took place at Lucas' Northern California studios, called "Skywalker Ranch.") The 1999 release of *Star Wars Episode I: The Phantom Menace* has convinced me that the *Star Wars* series, through cinematic storytelling, is quickly becoming a fundamental or underlying myth of our postmodern society.

Another is Steven Spielberg's *Jurassic Park,* wherein the heroes venture forth from the present day into a world of supernatural wonder, encounter fabulous forces, and finally return. Spielberg's 1998 film *Saving Private Ryan* is also in the mold of the Hero's Journey: A group of soldiers are sent on a quest to find Private Ryan and return him to safe haven. Lucas and Spielberg both understood completely the Hero's Journey model of Campbell through a book by Christopher Vogler, *The Writer's Journey: Mythic Structure for Storytellers and Screenwriters.* Vogler discovered Campbell as a young film student at USC. In his introduction Vogler pays tribute to Campbell and says, "In his study of hero myths Campbell discovered they are all basically the same story, retold endlessly in infinite variation." The "same story" means the universal three phases that we will explore in detail in Chapter 4. Vogler grasped the implications of the Hero's Journey and wrote his book to assist other screenwriters and storytellers in the proper construction of stories that engage and grip the reader or viewer. Over the years this book has been a conduit into Hollywood of the three phases of the Hero's Journey.

Further study of Campbell led me to two other important figures who must be mentioned: Carl Jung and James Joyce. Carl G. Jung, the Swiss psychologist, popularized the concept of archetype. Jung proposed that universal archetypes dwell in the subconscious minds of all human beings. Goliath, Grendel, Fishhook, and Darth Vader are clear symbols of the foe or enemy that are easily understood by children from Hong Kong to Greenwood, Arkansas. My stories about growing up in Greenwood contain the same universal symbolism as ancient epics such as *Beowulf.* Campbell was intimately acquainted with Jung's work, and eventually edited *The Portable Jung.* Campbell visited in Jung's home during his first trip to Europe in the 1920s. I would give my Stan Musial autograph to have been a fly on the wall that day as the young Joe Campbell asked Carl Jung about archetypes in the myths and recorded dreams from around the world. Furthermore, it was during this trip to Paris that Campbell was introduced to another important artist of the twentieth century who would have a powerful influence upon his thinking about myth and storytelling—James Joyce.

Joyce had just published the controversial *Ulysses* and young Joe picked up a copy from Sylvia Beach at her famous bookstore, Shakespeare and Company. He hurried to the nearest cafe to read the much talked-about novel. (In 1998 the Modern Library voted Joyce's *Ulysses* as the most important book of the twentieth century in the English language.) The next day the indignant young scholar stormed back into the bookstore and demanded that Sylvia Beach explain the book. *Ulysses* is, of course, Joyce's reinterpretation of the classic Hero's Journey, *The Odyssey*. Forty years later Campbell continued to use that same book—in very ragged form—in the teaching of his class on Joyce at Sarah Lawrence College.[1]

Jung, perhaps the most important psychologist of the century, and Joyce, arguably the most important literary artist of our time, understood the role of myth in our lives. It was Campbell who interpreted the work of Jung and Joyce to the American culture through his understanding of the universal role of myth.

The contemporary storyteller is a modern myth maker whether by means of film, novel, sitcom, poetry, or personal story.

Joyce believed a story was and is a symbolic piece of art that requires no commentary by the artist-storyteller. "Just tell them a story" is pure art; your commentary about the story is just your opinion, or what Joyce called pornography. We dare to differ from the great Joyce on this matter. The speaker's job is to persuade listeners toward his or her opinion, right or wrong.

[1]For a fabulous study of Campbell's teachings on James Joyce, see *Mythic Worlds, Modern Words: On the Art of James Joyce,* edited by Edmund Epstein. (Harper Collins, 1993).

Do not assume the three phases of the Hero's Journey work only in billion-dollar movie productions. Rites of passage are found not only in extraordinary tales of adventure, but in everyday experiences. Here are three examples of situations in which (I) the hero is separated from normal life, (II) crosses a threshold to face a supreme ordeal where transformation occurs, and (III) then returns triumphant:

1. A seven-year-old boy or girl with a Roy Rogers or Wonder Woman lunch bucket in hand (I) walks to school for the first day of class. (II) There, strange and mysterious forces are met which somehow change him or her. In the afternoon (III) he or she returns home, slightly different, walking with confidence, a real schoolboy or schoolgirl.

2. (I) A boy is taken from the village (separated) by the male elders. (II) He's placed in a hut; instructed in how to kill game, dress it, and cook it; shown how to prepare weapons; taught songs and stories; and (initiated) painted with stripes of the warrior-hunter. (III) He returns (integrated) to the village a man.

3. (I) A boy enters his first Little League game. (II) He walks to the plate to face the foe. (III) He returns home a ballplayer.

Learn to interpret daily events through a mythic sense. See the import of common events.

# 4 THE THREE PHASES OF THE HERO'S JOURNEY

Recently a speaker colleague asked, "Grady, can't there be four phases in this process?" My answer was and is, "It all depends." It depends on what we choose to call the four phases. We have already seen that the three primary stages of Hero's Quest mythology have their origin in rite-of-passage experiences common to all cultures around the world. It is possible that a thousand years of individual dreams eventually merged into community mythologies, folktales, and legends that have surprisingly universal themes and archetypal characters. Those myths or legends resonated with listeners around the campfire during storytelling sessions after dinner. The legends are filled with the separation-initiation-integration triad that flows out of the human experience. This ternary basis of human reality is discussed by Robert M. Torrance in this book, *The Spiritual Quest: Transcendence in Myth, Religion, and Science*. Torrance shows that in a diverse range of domains from myth to biology to religion to art, a three-phase process of growth, evolution, or movement is the common denominator. He writes: "As in every quest, every rite of passage, every physical and biological change is ternary." He states this partially in response to those who have viewed the basic human function as a simple binary process, or an overly simplified separation and return.

Although the thirdness is absolutely essential in movies, novels, and plays as well as personal stories, critics sometimes refer to stories as a binary process of separation-return, leaving the middle phase unstated. In his critical study, *Larry McMurtry and the West: An Ambivalent Relationship,* Mark Busby writes of McMurtry's work and suggests his themes as "escape and return, leaving and returning, looking to leave, and longing to return—the various versions of this double dichotomy characterize much of McMurtry's life and writing."

Busby refers to McMurtry's themes in only two phases. Perhaps in literary studies the binary motif is sufficient for understanding the overall theme of a particular writer's body of work. However, *Lonesome Dove* would not have been a popular novel or miniseries had Gus and the Captain been shown leaving Texas with their herd and arriving in Montana. The story is within the second phase, where a host of challenges are met including a desert crossing, Jake Spoon, river crossings, rustlers, hostile Indians, the archetypal villain Blue Duck, and more Indians in Montana. It is within the second—or middle—phase where movement from one place to the other is seen. In movement, the journey occurs.

It's possible to describe a story or a process as separation and return, but unfortunately there is no story there. There is no important initiation phase that changes or transforms the hero, who then integrates the newness into the old.

My speaking friend had been using a four-phase process to teach her theory on corporate change and had found it a very successful way to teach. She was emotionally committed to a four-phase process. After discussing her four-phase model it was clear to me that she was in fact using the traditional three phases, but was using the transformational phase that occurs inside phase two as a fourth and separate phase. In teaching the process of change or growth through the Hero's Journey model, it is acceptable to emphasize any phase you choose for your specific needs. This model is flexible to an infinite number, as seen by the hundreds of thousands of stories, novels, plays, films, and legends that have followed the three underlying stages while appearing unique and entertaining on the surface.[1]

Both Joseph Campbell and Christopher Vogler used the three primary phases, then added many subphases. Vogler used four subphases within each of the three primary phases, giving him twelve benchmarks for story production. Some of his subphases were refusal of the call, arrival of a mentor, and refusal of the return. Whether we prefer a binary process to explain human reality or four phases or even twelve, the fact remains that underlying those two, four, or twelve are three basic phases best described as separation-initiation-integration. As we will soon see, something very, very important occurs within the second phase that is the whole purpose of the Hero's Journey, and that something is transformation. However, that occurrence is so important that we will explore it separately in Chapter 5.

For our purposes as creators of personal story to use in speaking, a basic understanding of the primary phases is sufficient. Let's now separate the three phases and examine them in literature, cinema, and myth.

[1]In his continuing development of the spiritual growth guidelines of Meister Eckart, Matthew Fox has divided Eckart's theology into four phases. Not surprisingly, they parallel perfectly the processes of Torrance, the hypnotherapy of Erickson, and the Hero Journey phases highlighted by Campbell and others. Fox uses the Latin terms and describes the phases as: I. *Via negativa* (a breaking away or separation); II. *Via creativa* (a search and process of the new); III. *Via transformativa* (which we have placed within the second phase); IV. *Via positiva* (a coming together, return, or integration of the new).

## PHASE I. TAKE THE JOURNEY, OR SEPARATION

In his Pulitzer Prize–winning masterpiece *Lonesome Dove*, McMurtry names one of his co-heroes Captain Woodrow Call. (I've often wondered if the name Call has mythological significance for McMurtry.) One fine day the tight-lipped retired Texas Ranger approaches his lifelong sidekick, the charming, bantering Augustus "Gus" McRae (Robert Duvall's favorite role) and announces, "Augustus, we need to get a herd and go to Montana." The Captain is ready for a new adventure, and the reader (or the viewer—*Lonesome Dove* was made into one of the most successful television miniseries of all time) feels the call of adventure early in the story. In novels, movies, or stories told from the platform we feel a calling, as opposed to the more clinical term, separation.

Gus is very happy with his retirement in Lonesome Dove, Texas, where he plans to spend his golden years swigging from his jug and visiting Miss Lorena at the local saloon. So he initially turns down Captain Call. The story's first challenge is to get the co-hero to answer the call.

Every hero's journey begins with a call, a beckoning, perhaps an inner longing to strike out on an adventure. It is a quest for something that on the surface seems obvious—in this case, a new ranch and a new life in Montana—but when examined at a deeper level is actually unknown. The human need to take such journeys is instinctive. A man or woman of action cannot retire.

The underlying purpose of the journey is the process itself, and not a rigid, unwavering commitment to winning the prize. However, the process of transformation cannot occur unless the prize is sought.

The hero can refuse the call at first, as Gus does. Another example of the hesitant hero is Luke Skywalker, who wants nothing to do with war or being a Jedi Star Fleet fighter like his father, whom, he had been led to believe, was killed by the forces of the Dark Side. Luke is challenged by Obie Wan Kenobie to accept his natural calling as a Jedi and Star Fleet fighter. Luke refuses the call, but after returning home to find that the forces of the Dark Side have killed his grandparents and burned their home, he changes his mind, and the story begins in earnest as he crosses the threshold into Phase II, the great adventure.

Refusal is most often about fear. Not just physical fear—fear of the unknown or of great powers or forces that seem impossible to conquer. Fear of letting go of old, comfortable ways and habits, of our worldview, of our prejudices and defenses, of crutches such as drugs or alcohol.

Ultimately, the hero does indeed answer the call. Why? Because refusal to do so would lead to death by inertia.

Gus ponders his life in Lonesome Dove and secretly knows he needs a new journey, a new adventure. Every potential hero knows it's easier not to go. A part of us prefers to "get drunk," retire, play golf, be depressed, and do nothing, rather than to gather courage, seek new horizons, get involved in the world and the community, and move forward with optimism and enthusiasm. But heroes eventually overcome their reluctance. So Gus finally agrees to gather a new herd, hire young hands, and answer the call of the Captain. Audiences immediately identify with a movement toward a cause, a prize or goal. The very words "Once upon a time ..." will quiet a room full of energetic children. "I remember one time ..." is the beginning of a journey.

A storyteller engages the listener easily and immediately, then moves just as quickly to the second stage: facing the challenge. The challenge has also been called the nadir or the supreme ordeal.

## PHASE II: FACE THE CHALLENGE, OR INITIATION AND TRANSFORMATION

The second phase is the most important phase of the story, for it is within this phase where the challenges are met. I'll save the supreme ordeal and the idea of transformation—the purpose of the journey—for Chapter 5. Before going further, however, we must state that the three phases are models from which the savvy storyteller can veer and weave, surprising the listener, reader, or viewer. Understand the three phases clearly so that in the creation of your story you can be flexible and creative. In one story the call or beginning may be very brief and even unclear. In another story the third phase may be hidden in humor or couched in a surprise double ending.

The second phase is the true purpose of the story. Upon answering the call, the hero will soon face the first challenge. A threshold has been crossed, sometimes without the hero realizing it. The world around you has changed, or in the well-known words of Dorothy in the *Wizard of Oz,* "We aren't in Kansas anymore."

I can't imagine a story that more perfectly reveals the three phases of the Hero's Journey, especially the crucial second phase, than that of the film *Apollo 13.* Stories told in public speeches can be structured just as clearly as *Apollo 13* to reflect the universal three-part design of the Hero's Journey.

Here's how the real-life events of that epic adventure correspond to the three stages:

I.   Take the Journey: The blastoff of the Saturn rocket;

II.  Face the Challenges: The series of challenges leading up to the memorable words of Astronaut Jim Lovell (played by Tom Hanks in the popular movie), "Houston, we have a problem!" and including a symbolically perfect supreme ordeal during the tense reentry scene;

III. Victory: The successful return of the craft to Earth.

The heroes overcame one challenge after another, including a high fever that afflicted one of the astronauts, an explosion that could have hurled them into outer space (and did limit their ability to steer the ship), and an air filtering problem. After surmounting all those obstacles, they discovered a heat-shield problem. Reentry, always dangerous, became the greatest challenge of all, a supreme ordeal.

During several moments of blackout, viewers of the movie are left suspended, unsure about the astronauts' fate, just as many of us were when the events actually occurred. The tense moments of reentry blackout are a perfect example of a supreme ordeal—a life-or-death crisis in the story that defines the entire journey. The capsule survived reentry, the parachutes opened, and the transformed heroes returned home to Earth from whence they were launched.

*Apollo 13* shows how the second phase of the Hero's Journey contains the most important scenes. It is here that defeats occur, life-and-death ordeals are confronted, and transformation of the hero takes place. The astronauts of *Apollo 13* are given the opportunity to demonstrate even more heroic traits by overcoming challenges time after time.

Scott Greenberg, a popular young storyteller, speaker, and scriptwriter who has consulted on hundreds of screenplays in Hollywood, agrees that the second phase is the most important part of a story, movie, novel, or play. "It's relatively simple to launch a hero into a journey," observes Greenberg, "and it's not too difficult to bring him or her home and wrap it up. The trick in story creation is the middle phase wherein the most essential process occurs: transformation of the hero."

In fact, the second phase *is* the story, because the supreme ordeal is the point of a good story. "Fishook" begins with the little hero accepting the call to play in his first baseball game. When I tell this story, I feel a mood swing in the audience as we approach Phase II. Phase I is merely the setup. The audience is immediately transfixed, but interest heightens as we move into Phase II, which will lead to the supreme ordeal and transformation.

## PHASE III: FIND THE VICTORY OR INTEGRATION

The third and final phase of your story is the wrap-up, also referred to as the dénouement, a French word that literally means the "tying of the knot." The wrap-up of your tale serves as an anchor for your speech. Listeners should clearly understand the meaning of the story and the reason you have told it. Perhaps they will even visibly nod in agreement with you.

I call this third phase of the story Find the Victory. We find or interpret the victory of an event many years after the event actually occurred. At the time, the event may have seemed like a terrible ordeal or the definition of defeat itself. As we'll see in later chapters, humor often originates in these times of extreme embarrassment or failure. Not surprisingly, when we gather for family or class reunions, the stories we most often retell are of our valiant attempts to achieve great things, and how we were knocked down in the process. Failure is almost always recounted with humor.

Stories created for popular movies, such as Steven Spielberg's *ET: The Extraterrestrial,* the *Indiana Jones* series, and *Saving Private Ryan,* work best when the hero finds a clear-cut victory. But the speaker is telling a different kind of personal story, and the continuous clear-cut victory for the hero may cause the audience to resent the self-laudatory nature of a personal story.

Recently, I found myself growing more and more uncomfortable while reading the autobiography of a well-known woman writer, lecturer, and spiritual guru. I admire her intellect, oratorical skills, and other obvious talents and was puzzled at my growing irritation with her story. Finally, it hit me: She placed herself in the winning role in every episode of her life. She recounted dozens of childhood events wherein she was the obvious winner. Her brilliant humor, intellect, toughness, beauty, athletic prowess, and so on became the focal point of each of her stories. Annoyed at the narcissistic, self-adulatory tone of her writing, I finally tossed the book aside.

Moral of the story: If you want audience empathy or sympathy, don't tell them about your magnificent victories.

Nobody wins all the time. Though we long for Super Bowl trophies, rings, ribbons, statues, plaques, and big checks, many of our common-day adventures end in defeat. No one wants to hear speakers tell stories about how wonderful they are. Some of our stories are about winning, but the best ones are about the ordeals of the hero who somehow finds a victory even in defeat.

Our everyday lives are a series of challenges that must be joyfully overcome. Winning is our goal, but in reality we struggle, get knocked down in spite of our most heroic efforts, and somehow find the victory anyway. A great story is one in which the hero is determined to persevere until victory is won—or, more accurately, found.

U.S. Olympic skater Dan Janssen won a gold medal in speed skating. His story is compelling, touching, and inspirational, but it is not about winning a gold medal. It is about falling, about losing, about death and despair.

You may recall that Janssen was a multiple world-record holder and a big favorite to win the gold medal in Olympic competition from the late 1980s through the mid 1990s. In three different Olympic appearances, Janssen had skated into the finals, only to fall and go home empty-handed.

In 1994 he had one last chance for Olympic gold. But before he could focus on that, a tragedy worse than Olympic failure occurred: the death of his sister. A loving sibling with whom he had been very close through the tough years of Olympic setbacks was lost to him forever. With pressure far more intense than most of us will ever face, he went to the 1994 Olympic Games, hoping to redeem a lifetime of effort, training, and commitment.

In the 1500-meter finals, Janssen fell again.

With one event remaining, the 1000-meter finals, Janssen prepared himself for what he knew was his last shot at the prize. The gun sounded and off he went. He started fast, as he had done so many other times. He rounded the last turn and, with the whole world watching, streaked across the line in gold medal–winning time. It was a stirring moment, but it was made even more memorable by the failures of past attempts, and by his victory lap, during which he held in his arms his tiny baby daughter, who bore the name of his late sister.

The brilliantly talented woman who depicts herself as the victor in all her childhood stories not only irritates her readers, she reveals a deeper problem. She assumes that winning is the only payoff of an adventure and she is blind to the much deeper lessons taught by loss and failure.

Unlike the novelist who writes about the hero, the speaker is telling a story with one's self as the focus of attention. The listeners must be rooting for you to win or find victory and must be happy for you when victory is finally won. In order to gain their support and sympathy, the speaker must clearly show the pain, struggle, and failure in the events leading up to the final victory. Humor flows out of those continuous knockdowns, just like in a Three Stooges or Charlie Chaplin film. The Stooges, for example, were constantly trying to achieve a small success, but instead of reaching their goal, a series of hilarious knockdowns and defeats usually found them some small type of victory by the end.

The jester, trickster, or clown volunteers to play the role and freely invites the audience's laughter upon him- or herself. Heroes find the courage to laugh at their failed efforts for higher status, and the audience easily identifies with this human condition. Then, any victory at all is victory over defeat and the audience is able to rejoice in the shared experience.

This is the last stage of the journey, and of the story. Just as heroes return to share what they have learned, so must the storyteller now make known the purpose or meaning of the story. Certainly insights can be found throughout the story, but at the end the speaker must clarify and sharpen the meaning of the story.

Here are five examples of the third phase of return, integration, or victory.

1. Many critics feel the most memorable scene in the television miniseries *Lonesome Dove* was Woodrow Call's return of Gus' body back to Lonesome Dove.

2. Beowulf returned to his homeland after victory over Grendel, to rule as King for 50 years. He eventually died in a sacrificial battle with a dragon.

3. The space capsule of *Apollo 13* returned to earth after intense moments during reentry.

4. Ishmael returned to port after the harrowing battle with Moby Dick.

5. Dorothy returned to Kansas after her transformational visit to the Land of Oz.

The wrap-up or return is essential to the story. Whereas Phase II is the place of transformation and is the most important phase of the story, Phase III is where the point of the story is revealed. It's the payoff phase.

The storyteller is free to create new territory. While the three phases form the basis for effective storytelling, there are innumerable ways to rearrange, exaggerate, and emphasize different aspects of a story. Sometimes you can even break all the rules, as in the popular film *Thelma and Louise,* who drove over the edge of the canyon to their deaths rather than return and face the music. (Of course, this ending makes it difficult to produce a sequel.)

## What about a Heroine's Journey?

This question is inevitable and is usually asked very early in my workshops, which are quite often filled with women who are professional speakers, trainers, educators and even ministers.

There is no question that most hero myths center on men. Traditionally the adventurer was male, reflecting the accepted gender roles of ancient cultures. The males fought the battles, conquered other lands, slew the dragons, and served as "protector and servant"—the literal meaning of the word hero.

But obviously, there have been many, many heroic women through the ages, from Helen of Troy to Hildegard of Bengin to Rosie the Riveter to Hillary Rodham Clinton, who said she "would not be the kind of First Lady to stay home and bake cookies."

Women, too, can call upon their masculinity, or, as Jung put it, *anima,* to conquer and compete as vigorously as men.

On the other hand, men call upon their feminine side, or *anima,* to love, nurture and connect with their own children as well as with other communities and nations.

Both genders must balance masculine and feminine traits to compete and cooperate, to coerce and connect, to go for the prize while appreciating the process, to pursue a passionate goal as well as live fully in the present.

As we shall see later the testosterone inspired journey to conquer and win the prize is a necessary part of the human experience. Perhaps an even more important aspect of the hero's journey is to be transformed, tempered, and find balance as a more compassionate leader.

---

### Checklist for Speakers and Storytellers

1. Examine your personal stories for transformational value. Does the hero move from an original place to a better one?

2. Remember that the hero is not necessarily victorious in the story. He or she sets out to win the prize, but through the trials of the journey realizes he or she has been selfish or "I" oriented, and is then transformed inwardly to "We"-ness. Parzival was narrowly focused on his own desire to be a knight and a champion. He failed to recognize the Fisher King and further failed to ask the key question of the King, "What ails thee?"

3. Make the hero human. All of my personal stories are about me as a hero who "learns a lesson," and therefore the audience sympathizes with my character. If a speaker uses stories that show how talented or successful he or she is, the reaction of the audience will be resentful and resistant.

---

4. Strive for a moral or spiritual meaning. Stories that focus solely on gaining material wealth do not have the power of those that tell of a deeper quest.

5. Make sure the transformational value of your story is clear to the audience.

6. Look for stories in the supreme ordeals of your life. Divorce, death, loss, trauma, heartache, job loss, professional failures, and rejection all have something to teach. Were you humbled by these experiences and moved toward a more loving and compassionate attitude toward your fellow men and women? This is transformation.

# 5 TRANSFORMATION THROUGH LOSING AND LEARNING

_"Just win baby!"_
—Al Davis

_"He who loses his life will find it."_
—Jesus

George Lucas and Steven Spielberg have acknowledged their debt to the Hero's Journey model in their successful modern films such as _Star Wars_ and _Jurassic Park_. The hero leaves the ordinary world, enters into an uncommon world, faces major challenges, and returns. The hero does not always win. The hero is defeated at most every turn, learns, gets up, tries again, gets knocked down by the enemy, gets up, tries again, gets flattened again, learns some more, tries again, and this time faces a monster, challenge, or obstacles so huge that even the Ultimate Hero can't get out of this one—the Supreme Ordeal. But this time, somehow, having learned and changed in the process, the hero finds a victory.

Every hero lets go of his or her normal world, faces challenges, learns from those challenges, and returns a better person. From Luke Skywalker to Indiana Jones to Rocky to Beowulf to Parzival of King Arthur's court, we see heroes who faced major challenges, defeat, and death (both physical and symbolic); found the victory, sometimes in apparent defeat; and returned transformed and better leaders, more eager to serve than before.

The most effective stories are those wherein the hero faces a major challenge and is transformed forever because of the experience. I have used the term *nadir,* the low point of the cycle, to describe the seemingly impossible challenge. Christopher Vogler coined the more poetic term, Supreme Ordeal. Viewers of film and readers of great novels are engaged most when they see a clear-cut and gripping Supreme Ordeal. In his highly successful *Indiana Jones and the Raiders of the Lost Ark,* director George Lucas heightened the intensity of the story by moving a Supreme Ordeal to the very opening scene. The moviegoer, with popcorn and soda in hand has no sooner found a seat than we see the opening scene. Here are actual words from the shooting script. The script reads:

> Peru 1936
> Peru—High in the Jungle—Day
> Dense, lush rain forest. Eastern slopes, Andes. A narrow trail along the face of the canyon and a group of men make their way on it. At the head of the party is an American, Indiana Jones.

Lucas cuts to the chase in the very first scene of the movie. There is no call, no refusal of the call, no setup like we see in *Star Wars* when Luke must decide if he will answer the call. Within moments, Indiana Jones faces a series of seemingly impossible obstacles to overcome. He somehow survives and returns to the classroom, from whence he must immediately set out again on a new adventure in search of the ancient lost ark of the Hebrew people. *Raiders* is a continuing series of Supreme Ordeals that force the viewer to forego the popcorn and soda and become absorbed in the adventure. Indy becomes stronger with each challenge.

In your personal stories you will want to find and emphasize this kind of tension-filled conflict. The hero survives somehow and is transformed. Humor often arises out of the tension built up by the conflict and the defeat of the hero in that moment. In movies and novels, the viewer or reader is engaged or mesmerized by conflict. In storytelling the listener is most easily entranced by humor. Keep in mind too that our purpose is not to write or produce a movie but to create stories that will engage listeners in a powerful way.

## THE TRUTH ABOUT WINNING

Defeat of the hero is important. Defeat can become either tragedy or humor, whichever the storyteller chooses. My stories about growing up in Arkansas as the second son of the football coach are mostly about a quest for approval or higher status, and the subsequent defeat or failure, later turned into humor. The humor becomes the victory, or the retelling of the event many years later for the encouragement of the listener becomes the victory in that retelling.

In storytelling what happens to the hero in the midst of the quest is the very point of the story. The transformation becomes more important than the result of the contest.

Humans prefer a happy ending. We construct our art, movies, novels, plays, and stories around a heroic victory. In short, we want to be winners. Stories about winning inspire us to try again. We worship winners and winning. We quote Vince Lombardi, who said, "Winning isn't everything, it's the only thing."

But in reality we are well aware that in every race there are more losers than victors. At the colorful closing ceremony of the 1996 Olympic Games in Atlanta, we saw thousands of competitors who had dedicated years of their lives to winning a gold medal. Most of them failed. Are they considered losers? Of course not. The effort itself was a victory. The process *is* the prize.

A real hero—all of us who answer the call, which may come in the form of a divorce, a disease, a job loss, or life itself—sets out on a journey and encounters major challenges that force him or her to look inside, confront weaknesses, and break through to a transformation of the soul. Heroes are changed inwardly. They are humbled and return to their old lives more loving and ready to serve their fellow man. In the words of Joseph Campbell, the hero "returns to the village to share the boon."

That is the ideal story. For centuries, listeners have been experiencing something richer and deeper than outward victory or purely selfish grasping for the Holy Grail or the Prize, whatever it might be.

The real story of all our lives is not the few victorious moments when we are given an award, win the lottery, hit a home run, win a prize, buy a new home, get a raise, or watch the kids graduate. Those are wonderful moments, but they are the easy moments that we fantasize will last forever.

Real life is about facing the challenges that are so powerful and so strong that as adults we continuously seem amazed that life is treating us in such a horrible way.

Our personal stories are minimyths that contain within them the vast whole of every life and even of the universe itself. Every properly constructed story is the story of change and transformation from one way of perceiving life to another and better way. That's why refusal of the call is so devastating. Those who refuse transformation, change, and growth are psychologically, emotionally, and spiritually entrenched in their habitual place of perception and behavior. It can be said that those who refuse to change are addicted to a way of being. Addiction is refusing to let go and move on to new ways of being.

A person who chooses to journey moves from childhood perceptions of "reality," onward and inward to more mature viewpoints, values, and perceptions. Those who journey intellectually, spiritually, and emotionally as a way of life progress from narrowly focused assumptions about the righteousness of *our* village, community, state, and nation to more widely based views that other villages, communities, states, and nations also have merit. Refusing to move, change, search, and honestly process new information, like the church fathers of old who refused to look through the telescope of Galileo, is the most dangerous form of addiction.

From Greek plays to modern film, the Hero's Journey is essentially about the internal transformation of the hero as the external role unfolds. The internal story is about the loss of ego and the realization that loving, connecting with, and cooperating with thy neighbor is superior to conquering, killing, and competing with thy neighbor. In his book *Sacred Hoops,* former NBA Chicago Bulls Coach Phil Jackson describes how he slowly led the various individuals on the team from individual, big-ego, I-win/you-lose mentality, to a "we win together" concept. By deemphasizing the American notion of "just win (the prize) baby," Jackson was able to transform ten highly talented individual heroes (including Michael Jordon, Dennis Rodman, and Scottie Pippen) into a bonded team that focused on the joy of the process.

# THE HERO MUST LOSE AND LEARN

The childhood stories that I tell on the platform, including "Facing Fishook" and "Pine Tar," contain within them the essential element of struggle. The hero—me as a child—fails over and over again. Likewise, classic stories such as *Beowulf* and Parzival's story are excellent examples of the true underlying purpose of hero myths—namely, the inner transformation of the hero.

In *Beowulf,* which dates back to about 900 A.D., the great warrior travels to the kingdom of Hrothgar, arriving with much fanfare and celebration. He has come to conquer Grendel, the spirit monster who has wreaked havoc on the King's men for a decade. In the prebattle banquet and news conference there is much boasting and bragging about previous battles. Beowulf feigns humility, but the phrase "most eager for fame" appears in the text 16 times. His entire motivation is fame—and for that we do not fault the great warrior.

Muhammad Ali endeared himself to the entire world by shouting into the camera, "I am the greatest! I am the greatest of allllll time!" Beowulf-like modern professional wrestlers predict they will defeat the champion. Joe Namath guaranteed victory before playing in the Super Bowl.

Such boasting by warriors and athletes is indicative of the burning desire and giant ego necessary for high-level competition. Before the great battle the hero is self-absorbed, narcissistic, narrowly focused, and fanatically determined to win the prize at any cost. This catch-22 is necessary. The fanatical, narrowly focused, committed warrior whose purpose is victory at all cost will most often prevail in battle. Unfortunately, this is the very attitude that must be tempered and softened for the warrior to successfully relate to and live at peace with his fellow men and women.

That is exactly the message of Parzival, the young man who sets out with one goal: to become a knight. His search for the Holy Grail becomes a part of the story, but his primary focus is to become a knight. In his quest he eventually arrives at a lake where an old man is fishing. The old fisherman has received a terrible battle wound in his groin. He is in deep pain and his entire kingdom is under a dark curse. Parzival notices the wound but is so focused on his personal quest for knighthood that he quickly dismisses the old man's troubles and moves on in search of the Holy Grail.

Many years later, after overcoming numerous challenges, he once again arrives at the old man's castle. This time, the more mature, less self-focused Parzival notices the wound and says simply, "What ails thee?" With those words the wound is healed, the curse on the kingdom is lifted, he recognizes the old man as the Fisher King (for whom he has been searching for years), the Holy Grail appears, and Parzival becomes a knight. Like many heroes, Parzival set forth upon his quest so narrowly focused and determined to attain his own idea of the prize that he missed seeing it though it was right before his eyes.

Does the story of Parzival and the Fisher King teach us that goals are unimportant? No. But it does challenge us to rethink our goals and determine which are most important.

Goals are important, but even more important is maintaining balance and being connected to other human beings while we are on the journey toward attaining those goals. That's the underlying message of the Fisher King story. Parzival endured many years of hardship, learned many lessons, and experienced personal inner transformation. Not until then did he focus on the pain of others and take the time to inquire, "What ails thee?" In other words, only when the hero is changed inwardly, or transformed, is the quest fulfilled.

The same truth is found in *Beowulf.* Beowulf faces Grendel and defeats him in a horrific and bloody bout. There is a huge celebration, not unlike a ticker tape parade or a campus riot after a big bowl win. But the story is not over. While the celebrants sleep, a strange thing happens. Grendel's mother appears—about a thousand years before Freud—and devours a dozen warriors, then retreats back to her underwater den with Beowulf in hot pursuit.

Why Grendel's mother? In his book, *The Heart Aroused,* poet David Whyte aligns Grendel's mother with the real source of the problem. "At 3:00 a.m. after a day in the corporate world the real monster awakens us."

A vicious battle takes place with a monster stronger than Grendel, during which Beowulf fears he may have met his match. For the first time the champion warrior feels his mortality. He is down on the floor with a mighty monster on top of him who is about to cut off his head. In this Supreme Ordeal Beowulf reevaluates his priorities. Suddenly, his eyes are opened and he sees a powerful and well-known sword that he had not seen before (a hidden resource that is always there), grabs it, and quickly cuts off the monster's head.

We sense that the great champion is changed in this battle. There is less bragging after this battle and Beowulf, perhaps a little more humble, returns to his homeland where he serves his people justly for 50 years. Beowulf eventually meets his own death in a sacrificial battle with a dragon.

The real hero's quest is not about instant and glorious victory. It is about attempting to conquer something, getting your ears pinned back a few times, being slapped down by life's continuous obstacles, becoming stronger and stronger after each defeat, and growing inwardly so that the hero no longer thinks, "I must win the prize," but rather, "We will endure as a community together."

The Hero's Journey myths from cultures all around the world are trying to tell us something about ourselves as a species. They are saying, "Hey, human race, here's a hint! Perhaps there is a better way. Life is not only about I win/you lose. Life and culture can be about I win/you win."

The masculine in every man and every woman says, "I'll dominate you or you will dominate me and we will battle it out to see who wins. Mate it or kill it." But the feminine in every man and every woman says, "Let's embrace each other, nurture each other, hold each other in love."

The journey is about finding the proper balance between those two responses. Balance is the critical word here. Masculine and feminine styles are both very important. Finding the proper balance *is* the journey; especially for male. And that's why the Hero's Journey myths seem dominated by male heroes. The warrior-knight-hunter-hero male must find balance.

Perhaps we need go no further than home run king Mark McGwire for a metaphorical example of a hero conquering all and finding balance.

After McGwire, the giant 6'5", 245-pound slugger, stepped on home plate after hitting his 62nd home run, he scooped up his 12-year-old son and kissed him … on the lips. To paraphrase the words of Vince Lombardi, "Winning isn't everything; it's something that happens if you're fortunate after getting knocked down, being tackled, striking out, failing, and then getting up and trying one more time" *That* is the real Hero's Journey.

# EXERCISE

See if you can identify the Supreme Ordeal in the following well-known novels, myths, and films. Match the stories in the left column with the Supreme Ordeals in the right column.

| | | | |
|---|---|---|---|
| 1 | Star Wars | A. | "Use the force, Luke." |
| 2. | Apollo 13 | B. | Prehistoric monsters |
| 3. | Jurassic Park | C. | In the belly of the beast |
| 4. | Beowulf | D. | Reentry |
| 5. | Lonesome Dove | E. | Facing the great Oz |
| 6. | Jonah | F. | Battle with Grendel's mother |
| 7. | Wizard of Oz | G. | Gus McCrae facing the loss of his legs |
| 8. | American Graffiti | H. | Head on the chopping block |
| 9. | Back to the Future | I. | Of all the gin joints in all the … |
| 10. | Jaws | J. | Getting up off the mat one more time |
| 11. | The Fisher King | K. | Seven days under the Bodhi Tree |
| 12. | Braveheart | L. | Death at the drag race |
| 13. | The Buddha | M. | Pine tar on my fingers |
| 14. | Casablanca | N. | Future dad slugs the bully |
| 15. | Rocky | O. | Oxygen tank to the jaw |

16. Sir Gawain and the Green Knight

P. What ails thee?

17. Dances with Wolves

Q. Torture on the rack

18. Sophie's Choice

R. Imprisoned by the cavalry

19. The Unforgiven

S. Choice between children

20. Pine Tar

T. Beaten by the sheriff

(Answers 1A, 2D, 3B, 4F, 5G, 6C, 7E, 8L, 9N, 10O, 11P, 12Q, 13K, 14I, 15J, 16H, 17R, 18S, 19T, 20M)

This is not a scientific survey. You may disagree with some of my choices of the Supreme Ordeals in these stories. Feel free to disagree, for sometimes a multilevel story has more than one crisis moment.

# 6 FINGERPRINTS UPON THE UNIVERSE

When I finally understood the significance of the three phases or stages within the rite of passage of the Hero's Journey, a strange thing happened. The whole world seemed to divide itself up into threes. At first I thought I must be seeing things, or projecting my own awareness into other realities. As time went by I realized I was not just imagining the world in three parts.

After coming to terms with the three essential phases of hero stories I began to notice the three phases in other seemingly unrelated domains. First I saw it in the work of Milton Erickson. He told a brief story, anecdote, joke, or pun and brought the nervous patient into a safe area of "shared common experience." As a storyteller, I was naturally fascinated by Erickson's use of story to induce trance and his method of therapy.

Ernst Rossi divided Erickson's method into five stages:

1. Fixation and attention. (He used stories for a fixation point.)
   Once the patient is in a slight trance, the actual process of therapy begins at stage 2.

2. Depotenuating habitual ways of thinking and belief systems.

3. Unconscious search.

4. Unconscious process.

5. Hypnotic response.

As I pondered the five stages it was obvious that movement or journeying from one way of being to another way of being was the point of the therapeutic approach. Then it occurred to me that phase one, fixation, is not a part of the therapy itself, and the psychological movement or departure begins with depotenuating old or habitual ways of thinking, or separation. Erickson's stage 3, search, and stage 4, processing, are psychological parallels to the hero's crossing the threshold into initiation or transformation. Stage 5, hypnotic response, is the psychological equivalent of return, integration, wrap-up, or victory.

The Hero's Journey is clearly seen in Ericksonian hypnotherapy:

1. Leaving old habitual ways of seeing things or perceiving;

2. Search and process of new;

3. Integration of that new knowledge or way of seeing or perceiving.

A psychological journey and perfect parallel to every rite of passage. Satisfied that I was not forcing a square peg into a round hole, my observation of this pattern of threes grew even more keen.

Not long after reaching this awareness, I flew to Louisville, Kentucky to speak to a convention of health care workers who specialized in drug and alcohol rehabilitation. In flight I read some of the literature, which included the famous Twelve-Step Program. It became clear immediately that the 12 steps, which have become almost sacred to certain recovery groups, break down into the three clear phases: Steps 1 through 4 can be viewed as preparing to take the journey, or answering the call. Steps 5 through 11 can be summed up as making amends to those injured by one's addiction, a transformation phase. And Step 12 is volunteering to return and integrate by taking part in the recovery of others, or in Hero's Journey language, returning to the village to share the boon with your community.

When I mentioned this to the meeting planner he became flustered and, in hushed tones, made it clear that I should not mention my theory that the twelve steps could be summed up in three basic steps. Drugs and alcohol are not the only entities to which we can be addicted.

Those who refuse the call to journey, those who are in the habit of refusing to budge, fail to begin the journey, never face the challenge, and do not become heroes. They are addicted to habitual ways of thinking, perceiving, and believing.

In 1980, Marilyn Ferguson's book, *The Aquarian Conspiracy,* appeared in bookstores and became an immediate best-seller. Ferguson had written a masterpiece on the transformational change, documenting a great paradigm shift that was taking place throughout society. The book made sense of the continuing paradigm shift in which 75 million baby boomers then approaching their late thirties were engaged. I was too busy trying to be a comedian to read a book with such a far-out title. The Age of Aquarius had passed me by and, after years of Watergate, I was fed up with the word *conspiracy.*

It wasn't until 1991 that I read her book. As Ferguson began to unfold her thesis that a growing mass of people was presently bringing about a new way of looking at the world and our place in it, I felt strangely drawn to her work.

Transformation is a key concept in her book and, of course, is the major purpose of the Hero's Journey. I read faster and faster in search of the *how*. How are these people changing?

Finally I arrived at page 89: "Stages of Transformation." My heart was pounding as I read, and then, bingo. Jackpot!

Stage One:    Entry Point

Stage Two:    Exploration

Stage Three:  Integration

Stage One, Entry Point in Ferguson's terms is the call in Campbell's language, separation in more psychological language, and Take the Journey in my own interpretation.

Stage Two, Exploration in Ferguson's terms is synonymous with the search and process of Ericksonian language or, in my own term, Face the Challenge.

Stage Three, Integration is similar to return or wrap-up. The old is transformed into the new with higher status: Find the Victory.

The major thesis of the *Aquarian Conspiracy* is this: A large segment of the generation known as baby boomers ventured forth in quest of something deeper, faced challenges, were transformed by those experiences, and returned to bestow the boon on their fellows. The paradigm shift that began in the 1960s has been a cycle of change and challenges including the Vietnam War; experiences with psychedelic drugs; the inclusion of Eastern religions into mainstream culture; the struggle for equality for women, minorities, and gays; the growth of entrepreneurship; the emergence of awareness of the relational or contextual nature of reality; the questioning of traditional religions and emergence of new ways of experiencing life; the quest for meaning; and the strong interest in the environment. It is the journey of an entire generation.

It was becoming clear to me why our carefully crafted personal stories resonate within the soul of every individual and with society at large. Our seemingly unique personal experiences as heroic sojourners replicate and therefore resonate with all other sojourners as well as the present pattern of our entire culture.

## THE VERY FIRST JOURNEY

In the fall of 1991, armed with a new and deeper awareness of story power, I attended a workshop at Esalen Institute led by Richard Tarnas, who for ten years was director of programs at Esalen while researching and writing what would become a very special book. The workshop centered on that book, *The Passion of the Western Mind*. Little did I know that the book would quickly become a classic, that I was about to experience yet another life-shaper, and that my appreciation for the mind-boggling depth of the three phases would be, once and for all, anchored in my mind, heart, and soul.

Tarnas had worked closely with pioneers in the Human Potential movement, including Joseph Campbell, Abraham Maslow, Alan Watts, Michael Murphy (cofounder of Esalen and author of *Golf in the Kingdom*), Fritjof Capra (author of *The Tao of Physics*), and Stanislov Grof (author of *The Holotropic Mind*). Grof, a psychotherapist, is perhaps best known for his research into the birth experience as a foreshadowing of adult behaviors. Tarnas writes: "In the course of those years (ten as director of programs at Esalen) virtually every conceivable form of therapy and personal transformation, great and small, came through Esalen. In terms of therapeutic effectiveness, Grof's was by far the most powerful; there was no comparison." (p. 426)

What kind of therapy could be "by far the most powerful [with] ... no comparison?" Far beyond Maslow?

That got my attention.

Grof discovered that the deepest source of psychological problems reached beyond childhood memories, beyond even the earliest memories, all the way back to the actual birth experience itself. By taking hundreds of patients into their birth experiences, usually through some form of hypnosis, Grof studied their perinatal experience, and described it in the following way (as you read, keep in mind the three phases of separation, initiation, and integration): "In this context," says Grof, "certain crucial generalizations from the clinical evidence are relevant. First, the archetypal sequence that governed the perinatal phenomena from the womb through the birth canal to birth was experienced above all as a powerful dialectic—*moving from an initial state of undifferentiated unity* to a problematic state of constriction, conflict and contradiction, with an accompanying sense of separation, duality, and alienation; and finally moving through a stage of complete annihilation to an unexpected redemptive liberation that overcame and fulfilled the intervening alienated state—restoring the initial unity but on a new level that preserved the achievement of the whole trajectory."

What an incredible first journey for every little hero or heroine since time began!

Then I was struck by the obvious. The key words seemed to thunder into my consciousness: "from womb," "to birth canal," "to birth." One, two, three.

Look at the pattern: "moving from an initial state," "to a conflict," "sense of separation," "moving through a stage of annihilation," to "redemptive liberation," "restoring the unity but on a new level."

As I sat on the floor of the Grof House at Esalen and listened to Rick's carefully thought out and meticulous research, I felt a sense of completion and "getting it" that I had longed to experience since my first year as a seminary student. I knew immediately that the stories I had written and orally told to thousands contained within them the very heartbeat of life itself. By instinct I had crafted stories in three phases that parallel the first and most meaningful journey of every life. The connection of the properly constructed story was a connection with the Soul. It was beyond substance, beyond sizzle or humor; it was Soul.

The implications were staggering. The perinatal experience of every human being since the beginning of time has been a three-stage event, one that has had profound effects on later adult behavior. The event is so powerful that, according to Grof, adult behaviors such as depression, phobias, sexual disorders, obsessive-compulsive neurosis, and addictions might be explained and treated. Addiction? Hmmm, is it possible that some quirk of our unique birth experience may prevent us from accepting the call? Are some born to adventure, to journey, and others born to stay home and protect the status quo?

Our immediate concern is to explore the depths of story power, and we will not travel too far afield into the world of psychology. But before moving on we must deal briefly with an even more profound implication of the three phases, one that brings us very close to what I believe to be the very Fingerprint of God upon creation. Let's assume our unique perinatal experience is registered in each of us in several dimensions, namely, physical, psychological, intellectual, and spiritual. But wait! What we view as our unique birth experience may not be so unique after all. It appears that we encounter very similar phases of movement in our earliest human experience. And, writes Tarnas, "These experiences were profoundly archetypal in character."

Our rite-of-passage events, our dreams, worldwide myths, and our birth experiences are buried within our childhood stories. The stories we tell, from personal stories to *Star Wars,* resonate at the deepest soul level in every listener or viewer or reader. We have found the great Ah-ha! The aesthetic arrest that Joyce, Picasso, Da Vinci, and Spielberg strove for in their art is found in that place.

Tarnas continues: "Indeed, the encounter (in therapy as an adult) with our perinatal sequenced birth experience constantly brought home to subjects a sense that nature itself, including the human body, was the repository and vessel of the archetypal. Patients over and over again reported that the perinatal experience brought stark awareness of the universality of the process." In other words, patients in therapy sensed in their bodies all of creation and a unity or familiarity with the experience—a grand "ah-ha!" One center of all Aesthetic Arrest, an eternal "I'm here!"

Tarnas compares our birth experience, safe in the womb, suddenly head over heels down a constricted canal, out into a light, and on to a mother's breast, to "primordial Garden of Eden, the Fall and exile into separation from Divinity, followed by redemption through, once again, a death-burial-resurrection."

During the weekend workshop I talked at length and somewhat excitedly with Tarnas about these implications. I was thrilled to learn more and more of Tarnas' theories and will allow the book, which is now a classic, to speak for itself. In general, Tarnas theorizes that the entire scope of the human drama, especially the Western mind, can be viewed as a birth experience. Humankind has: (I) separated from its source (seen as a Fall); (II) faced the challenges of a species on a long, perilous, evolutionary and cyclical journey; and (III) is now in the process of reunification with the source. In fact, humankind may be in this period of history facing the nadir, the Supreme Ordeal, as consciousness attempts to move to the next level.

Dr. Kathyrn Cramer, a psychologist and author of *Staying on Top When Your World Turns Upside Down,* pointed out that this may be the first time in the history of the West when a critical mass of the population, baby boomers and the Aquarian Conspiracy, is approaching 40 (now 50) years of age, going inward, at the same moment that Western history may also be on a parallel journey. Tarnas agreed with her assessment and in fact was very intrigued by the idea.

I came away from the Esalen workshop with a much deeper understanding and appreciation for the relationship between mythology, psychology, and theology. The three stages of story, of psychotherapy, of novels, movies, the Hero's Journey of an entire generation of people, our unique birth experience and indeed the continuing, ongoing, death-burial-resurrection of everything, is a brush with eternity. This hint from beyond about how things work, how life works, seems to me a clear voice, an easily seen and clearly understood pointer and direction indicator upon which we find the very Fingerprint of God.[1]

## SUMMARY: PART I

1.  Hero's Journey stories from around the world contain three basic phases: separation, initiation, and

---

[1]For a detailed discussion of the Tarnas Theory, see Ken Wilber's *Sex, Ecology, Spirituality* (Shambhala Press, New York–London, 1993). In his notes he discusses (page 751) the possibility that western civilization is in the midst of a macro-cycle, a three-phase journey now in the supreme ordeal phase; therefore transformation from one way of being (rational), to another higher level (transrational). Wilber does not totally agree with the Tarnas thesis.

integration; or Take the Journey, Face the Challenge, Find the Victory.

2. Effective stories in a speech must contain the same three phases in order to work properly. There are a million variations, of course, but your story will work best if the three phases are present. There are potentially dozens of subphases. Refusal of the call, the arrival of a helper, a false start, getting side-tracked, and refusal of the return phase can all be part of a movie, novel, miniseries, myth, or legend. Our personal stories are probably simplified versions of hero myth stories; but sometimes, as we will see in "Facing Fishhook," they can become multilayered and complex, with many subplots and sidetracks.

3. All phases are important. Phase II, wherein the hero faces the supreme ordeal, is the most important.

4. The hero may "win" in classic style, like Beowulf, or the hero may face more tests, like Parzival. In personal storytelling the hero often fails, gets knocked down, then later retells the tale of defeat for humorous effect. The "win" or "victory" in that case lies in the recounting of the tale years later for the edification and inspiration of the live audience. We Find the Victory in the courage to create an artistically told story out of a painful or tragic event.

5. Your audience universally recognizes archetypes within your story: the hero; the mighty foe, like Goliath or Grendel; a mentor, like Obie Wan Kenobie. You may not be aware of the psychological implications of your story. I wonder if Herman Melville really understood the psychological depths of *Moby Dick*? He wrote his classic hero tale long before Freud uncovered its meanings.

6. Good stories are often rite-of-passage events, but not always. There are exceptions to every rule and rules are made to be broken. For example, *Dubliners,* by James Joyce, arguably the greatest storyteller of this century, consists of a series of sketches that do not have a beginning, middle, and end. Joyce's classic works *Ulysses* and *Finnegans Wake* are developed around the hero motif of Homer's *Odyssey.* Sherwood Anderson's, *Winesburg, Ohio,* is a series of sketches. My all-time favorite, William Saroyan, today a neglected genius, used varied types of stories in his many wonderful books.

7. Humor flows out of rite-of-passage events gone awry, incidents that were painful or embarrassing at first but are later interpreted as humor.

8. Take the Journey: The courage to go, to answer the call assures an eventual victory of some kind. Without the courage to take the journey, there is no story to tell.

9. Face the Challenge: Life is about challenges and overcoming them, getting knocked down, and trying again. The hero's journey myths, novels, and films—especially modern films—usually show the hero in a clear and fabulous victory. In real life, however, the hero most often fails many times before eventual transformation or victory. Your stories can demonstrate this reality and do so with humor.

10. The supreme ordeal can be physical, psychological, emotional, or spiritual. It should be clear and should be the focus of the story.

11. In transformation, the hero grows, learns, and gains something, but not for his or her own selfish use. Transformation is the purpose of the journey. The

hero may win or lose in the traditional sense, but in reality the hero wins just by taking the journey. He or she will never be the same.

12. Find the Victory: We learn from classic stories such as Parzival, *Star Wars,* and *Lonesome Dove* how we can use personal stories in speaking. The victory may be cloaked in lessons, morals, insights, and even humor.

# DISCOVERING AND DEVELOPING YOUR STORY

---

*"The first ingredient of successful therapy, taught Freud, is the remembering of forgotten aspects of childhood experience."*

—Mark Epstein M.D., *Thoughts without a Thinker*

# 7 STEPS ONE AND TWO: THE STORYBOARD OF DISCOVERY

Recently my brother, sister, and I took the time to separate ourselves from our families and normal routines to spend the weekend together. It was a reunion of siblings. Immediately, we were deep in conversation about our childhood days in Greenwood, Arkansas, sharing stories about schooldays, friends, neighbors, our parents, kinfolks. We also discussed religious beliefs, meanings, and values and how those have changed since childhood. Many of the stories were filled with peals of laughter, or "Can you believe that?" and "Do y'all remember the time?"

As we passed the weekend sitting in the middle of the lake on a pontoon boat with snacks and wine, it became obvious that I claim to remember far more childhood events than David or Jane do. We were somewhat amazed at how different my version of certain events seemed to be. David, the oldest, remembered fewer of the events than Jane or I, and continuously rolled his eyes and said, "Wow! I don't remember that at all."

Of the 30 or so of my stories published in *Sports Illustrated,* the vast majority of them were about childhood events. Why is it that these childhood stories resonate with audiences? Dan P. McAdams writes in his book, *Stories We Live By,* "At a very early age we begin to form a personal theme, a personal mythos for our lives that becomes self-defining; our personal story." The stories we tell generally arise out of this central theme. McAdams says, "About the age of ten, real-life motives began to form." We pick and choose our own style of how we will get what we want out of life from the behaviors we observe and absorb from our environment.

It is in childhood that we become who we are going to be as adults—or, from acorn to oak tree. When we tell stories about our childhood experiences, our audiences begin to understand *why* we are *who* we are. My role as second son has been a major influence in my life. Important modern research reveals that birth order plays a critical role in our personality formation. Northwestern University professor Frank Sulloway's book, *Born to Rebel,* is a landmark study in birth order. His thesis is that second children and later-borns are deeply affected by their places in the sibling pecking order, and that this imprinting occurs very early in childhood.

My speaking career has been built on the premise of being the second son of a football coach. My brother, David, doesn't have this identity. As the firstborn, his experience was far different. He was also successful in sports, made good grades in school, and in general moved through adolescence smoothly. His very existence was a daily reminder to me of my shortcomings. Your identity will be quite different from mine, but nonetheless defined to a great degree by your role in the family unit. Maybe you were the youngest and could do no wrong. Perhaps you were the only child of substance-abusing parents. All of these circumstances affect your identity and, thus, your story.

Most people can recall childhood events, especially when prodded by listening to others tell of their first bicycle or first Little League game or special Christmas or birthday. But more people than you might imagine confess they have little or no memory of childhood events. Maybe they just don't have good recall, but it's more likely they have blocked past events that they choose not to recall. After all, childhood is not the carefree, idyllic time that we often try to make it appear later in life. Psychologist Alice Miller writes in her book, *Drama of the Gifted Child* (Basic Books, 1996), that childhood can be the most painful and heartbreaking time of our lives. I recently read again Miller's book entitled *For Your Own Good: The Roots of Violence in Child-Rearing* (Virago Press, 1980), and I was reminded of the potential trauma of childhood experiences inflicted upon small children by well-meaning parents. Someone has suggested that human beings spend their entire adult lives trying to come to terms with childhood trauma. And that's exactly why childhood stories are so gripping and connecting for human beings.

Why I choose to remember vast numbers of childhood events in colorful detail we may never know for certain. David and Jane often say, "I can't believe you can remember all that stuff!" Well, I really can. The details live in my mind, the sounds, smells, color, and even the feelings and emotions that were in my heart at the time: the first day of school, the Canary reading group, facing Fishook, playing football, sitting all day in the high school gym as a 4-year-old watching Daddy coach basketball and teach volleyball PE classes, working in the garden, riding the school bus, being in church, climbing the trees in the backyard, taking long car trips to Fort Smith (almost 15 miles away), and on and on and on. When I tell these stories on the platform I am not just telling the story; beyond showing the event, it is as if I am reliving the event as it happened.

## REDISCOVERING YOUR STORY

When I conduct story development workshops it becomes obvious after a short time that some people recall childhood events more readily than others. First, I ask attendees to write out a list of memory joggers. For example, I say "Write down a list of all your birthday parties, or all your first days of school at various grade levels, or first boyfriend or girlfriend," and so on.

I first started doing this with groups several years ago and was not always happy with the results. I assumed it was because I was suggesting the list and participants felt coerced to remember events that I thought might be of significance. Then I stumbled onto a method that I now use with great success: the storyboard. It's simple, but profound in its results.

The storyboard exercise is the easiest and most powerful method I know for digging into the past and suddenly reconnecting with or remembering important, self-defining events from childhood that can very quickly be developed into high-impact stories and eventually even a signature story. Here's how it works.

### Step One: Creating a Storyboard

Get a piece of typing paper or, better yet, a big piece of white poster board. You can work off this storyboard for years if you choose to. Locate some colorful felt-tip pens.

Now, draw the floor plan of your childhood home. Pick out the house you recall the most fondly around the age of 8 to 10. In simple line drawings, sketch out the floor plan of kitchen, living room, bedroom, your parents' bedroom, front porch. In the lower right-hand corner, draw a stick-like picture of your school building. It's amazing how much of our childhood formative moments occurred in school. In the lower left, draw a significant place in the yard, front or back: a tree, a swing, or a big rock where you played.

In the upper right, draw a symbol or icon representing where your values and beliefs were formed. Your values may have begun in a childhood place of worship or religious training, a church or synagogue or mosque or wherever. Feel free to be creative. There is no need to be tied to a method. It's your childhood, it's your experience.

If you grew up in a city, you may not have had your own tree. So, draw the steps leading up to your apartment or where you played with friends. If you grew up on a ranch in New Mexico, draw a corral or barn. If you were a fisherman's child in Maine, you might draw a picture of your dad's fishing boat. Create a storyboard of your life.

## Step Two: Remembering Childhood Events

All set? Now, spend some time placing special objects in the rooms: chairs where Dad and Mom sat, kitchen table, beds, a TV. Strangely enough, very few scenes pertaining to the TV have ever entered my mind. Why? We didn't have TV until I was about 8 years old and my self-defining story was already deeply embedded. Yours may be quite different from mine.

Consider the drastic difference between my childhood, before television, and my own son's childhood. The pre-TV generation played outside, made up games, climbed trees, hiked to the creek, played kick the can—all outdoor activities. The post-TV generation watched television and played video games and today spend countless hours in the virtual unreality of the Internet. How this will affect their lives we don't really know. But you can rest assured—it will!

Oddly enough, as I ponder the vast generational gulf—and therefore the stories that will emerge—between my childhood and my son's, I can see that our differing cultures will affect our stories. Whereas my stories originated in a culture predominantly influenced by World War II, an America of 50 years ago, his childhood stories will be of another time. His rite-of-passage moments have been more about Legos™ than swimming holes, Super Mario Brothers rather than the Marx Brothers, and Mr. Rogers instead of Roy Rogers. His generation has never heard of kick the can or a party line (except in Congress), nor have they experienced an old-fashioned typewriter or heard of polio.

When my son begins to tell his childhood stories, chances are his will be filled with tales of Homer Simpson and his "Pine Tar" anecdote might feature rollerblading rather than playing basketball. Either way, his personal perspective will resonate with the audience if he understands the context and follows the basic format of the Hero's Journey.

Now, add other objects from your unique history to your storyboard. As you move your eyes from room to room you will be surprised at the flood of long-forgotten scenes and events. Strong and powerful events are just below your conscious level of awareness, and as you stroll around your childhood home, you'll be amazed at the scenes that surface. Some will be happy, some will be sad, some will be slightly painful. Some may be extremely unpleasant or even shocking. Remembering childhood events is a powerful psychological process. Many of the events you recall may be traumatic, but these are the life-shapers that may eventually turn into strong signature stories.

As these events pop into your mind, choose a colorful felt-tip pen and draw a small symbol of that event, like an icon on the computer screen. Later, when you prepare to use this story in a speech, you will simply place the icon on your note card or speech outline and tell the story. Don't worry about remembering the details just yet. We're going to develop the story properly in Chapter 8.

Look for events that might be described as rite-of-passage moments. Any event that contains the three phases of separation, initiation, and integration is potentially a good story. The most memorable stories are those about rite-of-passage events that went awry. A rite of passage gone wrong can later be viewed with humor and may be the basis for an entertaining story in your speech.

Be as creative and elaborate as you please. You may choose to place funny events in red, sad events in blue, and so forth. Obviously, very few of these icons are going to make it into a speech or program. But that very special event is in you somewhere, and we're going to keep looking until we find it.

In my workshops, we pause at this point to share icons. The results are always highly entertaining and sometimes even sad. In a recent workshop, a Boston woman told about the day she and her sister made too much noise washing dishes in the kitchen. Her father scolded them to keep it down. Then he began to complain of chest pains and later died. She was shocked that 40 years later, that scene came back to her in a flash simply because she gazed at her floor plan.

On another occasion, a participant drew a tree in the lower left corner. "What does that tree represent?" I asked.

"Oh, nothing important," she said.

"Want to share what it means?"

The moment she began to tell us about the tree and its meaning, she exploded into tears. The tree symbol carried tremendous emotional weight for her. As a child, she had sought shelter and peace in that tree from a verbally abusive father.

Another memorable moment in storyboarding occurred when an attendee drew a series of tobacco pipes throughout her childhood home. The pipes belonged to her father, who would arrive home after work each night, settle into his favorite chair, and spend hour after hour filling his pipe with tobacco, carefully tapping it down, lighting and puffing and relighting as pipe smokers do. "And what are you feeling about those pipes and your father?" I asked.

There was a moment of hesitation. Then she said, " I sat down at the end of the couch and secretly wished that my father would hold me and caress me and love me the way he did those pipes." She later retrieved one of those pipes from her mother and developed a powerful story around it.

Here are some examples from my own storyboard that might help jog your memory:

- The gray Formica-top kitchen table, and chairs with red snap-on seats that occasionally came loose and dumped the surprised victim on the floor.

- The outdoor basketball goal that Daddy put up. I felt that it was David's goal but I could play around it too.

- Our bedroom walls covered with pictures of major league baseball players; I recall Warren Spahn, Art Mahaffey, Sandy Koufax, Don Drysdale, Mickey Mantle and Bob Gibson and, most important of all, a picture of Lance Alworth, Arkansas Razorback All-American. (I remember the exact pose of each player, and the uniform colors.) This memory is significant in that my entire youth was shaped by hopes, dreams, and aspirations of athletic achievement. Naturally, I was unaware at the time that much deeper motives (there's that word again) were connected to my need to earn the approval and blessing of my father, the Coach.

Other significant areas and icons that jog my memory are:

- My parents' tiny bedroom, where as a little boy I often crawled in bed with them.

- The tie rack where my father's ties hung, already tied for Sunday morning. That tie rack hangs in my closet as I write these words.

- The bookcase in the living room that I climbed, up to the top shelves. I spent a lot of time seated in the corner looking at books. I clearly recall certain pictures.

- The house behind our house, filled with interesting junk.

There are three reasons I focus on childhood stories.

1. Because they are rite-of-passage events, which are universal and therefore resonate with every listener, breaking all barriers such as gender, age, race, religion, region, and politics.

2. Because personal childhood stories are self-revelatory in nature. Self-revelation is an important part of bonding with an audience. Who is the person speaking to us? What does this person think, believe, feel, and know that might be of importance to me?

   Childhood events reveal the making and shaping of the adult who stands before the audience to tell the story. That is not to say adult stories are less effective. They can be powerful, but it is more likely that someone in the audience will not identify with an adult story due to the natural diversity that occurs in adult life. As adults we separate into groups that can cause serious barriers in communication. We make choices; we become Democrats and Republicans, liberal or conservative, Christian or Buddhist, or whatever. As a southern male, I have occasionally been prejudged as a male chauvinist. These are differences, perceived or real, that can create a chasm between the speaker and the audience.

A childhood experience takes the audience into a more universally acceptable place of being. The audience is more accepting of the story and less likely to question the speaker's ideology or belief systems.

3. Personal childhood stories are fun. They are fun to create and they are fun to tell. Don't underestimate the importance of fun. Corporate speeches are notoriously boring and cold. There is an atmosphere of no-nonsense flowing out of a bottom-line mentality that prohibits fun. A corporate executive who injects fun, humor, and play into the presentation can break down—or perhaps melt down—the barrier between executive and employees. From Ross Perot to Ben Cohen and Jerry Greenberg of Ben and Jerry's ice cream, a host of executives dare to risk "not being taken seriously." The risk has a great payoff: By using fun, humor, story, and vernacular language, they win over the hearts and minds of listeners.

I have seen some amazing storyboards during our workshops. Childhood comes to life and memories of long-lost scenes and events flood the mind as participants dig into the subconscious for very important and sometimes life-shaping scenes, events, moments, and experiences.

## Outside the Floor Plan

Before moving to Step Three, which takes us into the domain of development, let me encourage you now to move out of the floor plan. The storyboard is a solid beginning, but as I reflect upon my own stories, I realize that it is only a beginning. Many of my stories occur outside the childhood home.

My most popular published story was called "The Once in a Lifetime Dive" when it first appeared in *Sports Illustrated* and *Reader's Digest*. Today it is called "Snickers and Snakes" in *Chicken Soup for the Sports Fan's Soul,* and it took place at our favorite swimming hole. "Facing Fishook" happened at Lions Park in Fort Smith, Arkansas. "Pine Tar" took place at the high school gym. "The Canary Reader" took place in my second grade classroom, the "Jazz Kittens" in the high school auditorium, and the story I call "Sunday Morning" took place at home in the kitchen and later at church. I could go on and on. Don't be tied to any one particular place. All of the scenes and places mentioned above are significant localities in my childhood: home, church, school, ballfield, swimming hole, and so forth.

### Other Resources

*Personal Journal.* I am an avid journal writer. Almost every significant event of my life during the past ten years is recorded in a computer journal. Many of those events are of very little interest to anyone but me. But occasionally, when I read through my journal notes, an event appears that could be a great story.

*Picture Albums.* Recently at Homecoming weekend in Greenwood, Arkansas, the class of 1949 looked through three thick photo albums compiled by my brother David. These albums were filled with team pictures and newspaper clippings from the 1946–47 football and basketball seasons. Memories, events, and stories poured from the class members as they thumbed through the albums.

*Home Video.* A more modern source of stories is the home video. This is a relatively new gold mine of scenes and events for future story creators.

*Community Memory.* While seated at the coffee shop during the Homecoming weekend mentioned earlier, I was entertained by local storytellers who told hilarious tales about their own childhood days. Many of the stories originated around my grandfather's farm and were rich in humor and human drama.

## Writing It Down

Writing has been a form of therapy for me. The hour-by-hour writing out of hundreds of childhood scenes have, for years, been the most meaningful, psychologically soothing, emotionally compelling, and spiritually uplifting hours of my life.

During more than two decades of writing almost every day, I can't recall a single time that I didn't come away from the yellow legal pad, typewriter, or computer emotionally high, with a feeling of deep satisfaction and accomplishment. Twenty-five years ago as a fuzzy-cheeked minister, I began to write down scenes from my childhood. As many as 50 of those stories have been written and rewritten, gradually evolving in preparation for publishing.

When I began speaking professionally in 1979, these stories were in the early development stage in writing only. From that time forward, they evolved in both written and oral form. As we'll see later, a written story is dramatically different from an orally developed story. But what they have in common are the three phases of the hero's quest. I was not aware at the time that the three phases, sometimes ever so subtly, were contained within my own stories. Fortunately, you now have the formula to make your own stories successful.

How many times have you heard the following: "I wish I had written down (or recorded) my grandmother's stories"? It's time to get serious about developing your stories.

Here's how: Choose one of the icons or symbols on your storyboard. Take a moment to identify the three phases. (I

Clarify the call or the moment the journey begins. It doesn't have to be perfect, but try to find that moment. Then, (II) see if you can identify the threshold crossing into challenges and find the Supreme Ordeal. Within the Supreme Ordeal is probably what you remember most about the scene or event you have recalled and listed on your storyboard. The Supreme Ordeal contains the real emotional power of your story.

Finally, (III) envision a victory, payoff, or wrap-up. It doesn't have to be funny at this time. It's just a memorable childhood event.

With the three phases in mind, it's time to write the story. It is very likely that the written version will evolve and your final version that is delivered live in front of an audience will be dramatically different. That's why it's called a process.

Write it out briefly, in fewer than a thousand words. Think about writing it for *Reader's Digest.* You may write out the bare facts; no need for embellishment or exaggeration. On the other hand, you may wish to go for it! Be outrageous and see what happens. It is unlikely that the first draft of your story would make it into *Reader's Digest* anyway, so the pressure's off! I clearly recall reading a story of mine to a gathering of friends and family all huddled in the kitchen. By the end of the story, the kitchen was empty. The story was later successfully published and has become one of my signature stories. But it sure was a clunker the first time around. By *signature story* we simply mean a story that is powerful, funny, and successful with every audience—a real keeper. *Signature story* can also mean a story that is uniquely a part of the storyteller and would not translate to another storyteller. The story is identified with the teller.

Unfortunately, every story may not be a final keeper. I have dozens of stories in my files that at one time seemed great but, alas, failed to make the cut. The only way we can find the final keeper that will become a signature story is to unearth a dozen or so.

How will you know a keeper when you see it? The answer to this question will be made clear in Part III, Delivery. It's easy to become discouraged at this phase of creating a story, because it's almost impossible to know whether it's good or not. Your story may not come to life until it is told to a live audience. That's the simple answer to the question, "How will I know if it's a keeper?" At the writing stage there is a burst of enthusiasm and hope for the potential power of a story. Then we work with it a while, and it usually seems a little less powerful.

Let's move on to further development of our story.

# 8 STORY DEVELOPMENT: FROM HUMBLE ORIGINS TO ART

L et's look now at one of my stories, from the event itself to writing to oral delivery. "Facing Fishook" evolved during 15 years of oral delivery in both stand-up comedy clubs and professional speaking. In the oral version of this story there are many, many laugh lines. This written version is ... well, I hope you find it amusing.

"Facing Fishook" is based on one incident in my first Little League game, a rite-of-passage experience that every southern boy was expected to endure. In those days no one had thought of the idea of making sure all the kids were the same age. I was eight years old and David was nine. He would pitch and bat cleanup. With Big Dave in the line-up I figured we would win the whole tournament in spite of a strange rumor circulating in the car about the opposing team, something about a fish hook—which turned out to be Tommy "Fishook" Smith.

I must remind the reader that a written version of orally constructed and developed story material is dramatically different from its oral counterpart. Read this story and later we'll compare "Facing Fishook" with a particular Arthurian legend, "Sir Gawain and the Green Knight." You'll be intrigued by the archetypal parallels.

## "FACING FISHOOK"

"James," Daddy suddenly barked at me in that tone that made me wonder if he was mad at me for playing with sister Jane on the kitchen floor, "better find your ball glove, Hoss. You're gonna be in right field tomorrow."

It had finally happened. I would be playing in my first real baseball game on a real field in the exciting Pee Wee League Tournament. It was impossible to sleep that night, thinking about playing in a real game with David and the other boys.

During the long drive to Fort Smith, I sat in the back seat and pounded my fist into my Stan Musial glove and listened to the gang talk and laugh. And then, yes, that word again, something about a fish hook. Why a fish hook at a baseball game? From what I could gather from the talk of the older and much more worldly boys, a Fishook scare happened at the plate when you batted. I had never batted in a real game before, so there was much to learn.

As we piled out of the car and ran for the field, I told Daddy that I would not be going to the plate to bat. "I'll play outfield, Daddy, but I don't want to bat."

He glanced at me and said, "You'll do fine, son. Get up there and take your cuts. Be a little man."

I told some of the other kids that I was not going to bat. Big kids could throw the ball real hard and it made a buzzing sound when it came near you. Playing outfield and catching fly balls was fun and I knew I could catch fly balls if they weren't too high and I could throw the ball back in to the infield, but I didn't like the idea of batting against a complete stranger.

Joe Stafford, one of my best friends, had a cousin in Barling, Arkansas whose name was Tommy Smith. His older brother was Hal Smith the actual catcher for the St. Louis Cardinals where Stan the Man played. It was hard to imagine that a kid from our area had a brother who played major league baseball, but it was true. Hal Smith's little brother, Tommy, was also a great baseball player, and they called him ... Fishook.

So, that was it. What an odd nickname, I thought. Naming a guy after fishing equipment probably meant that he really liked to fish, like my Daddy, and fished so much that his friends started calling him Fishook.

"Fishook?" I laughed and said, "What a funny name!"

I sat on the bench in the real dugout under lights and pounded my fist in the Stan Musial glove and thought about catching high fly balls and the chocolate malt that I would get at the Dairy Delight after the game. Greenwood didn't have a Dairy Delight, but when we came to the big city we sometimes stopped by the Dairy Delight for ice cream cones. Daddy called them a "cone a' cream." I had twenty-five cents in my pocket for something much better than a cone a' cream, a big chocolate malt.

Lions Park had a grass infield, an outfield fence, a real backstop, and stands where the mothers sat, white lines on the baselines, real bases, umpires in blue suits, and white baseballs.

I didn't know we were playing Barling, Arkansas, where Joe's famous cousin was from. Joe seemed to know everything before everyone else, so when he looked across the infield to the other bench and spotted his cousin Fishook, he wasn't too surprised.

"There he is," Joe said and pointed across the diamond. David and some of the other older boys looked at the other bench. I looked too and saw for the first time Tommy

Fishook Smith. He wore a baseball uniform with a red-sleeved shirt and red baseball cap. He wore red socks and black baseball spikes. He was very, very big and had a dark complexion. His jaw bulged with a chew of tobacco and he spit on the ground and scratched at his crotch and made noises. I was glad I would not be batting.

The game was about to begin. Fishook walked to the mound and threw a warm-up pitch. It streaked to the plate in a blur and slammed the catcher's mitt. Thwapp!! David and Joe looked at each other and their eyes got big and even my brother Dave said, "Wow!"

I walked over to Daddy and said, "Daddy, I'll play outfield but I don't want to bat."

He was smoking his cigarette and looked out to the mound where Fishook warmed up.

"Jamesey, if you're big enough to play outfield, you're big enough to bat."

Daddy didn't seem to understand that I would not be batting. He said I was batting ninth. I looked out to where Fishook pawed at the mound and spit tobacco juice. He snarled and was already sweating. He had hair on his thick brown arms and needed a shave. He was a man.

The first pitch rocketed to the plate and slammed into the mitt. Strike! The umpire said.

Daddy was coaching at third base. "Take a cut boys, you can hit him. Time it right. Here we go."

Three batters walked to the plate, faced three pitches, and walked back to the dugout.

"Wow, you oughta see that hook!" Earl Terry roared after striking out.

"What hook?" I said.

"Fishook's hook!"

Oh, so that's why they call him Fishook. A hook pitch. But, what could that be?

I ran to right field as fast as I could run and stood in my place. From way out there I could see all our mothers sitting in the stands behind the screen back stop. When I arrived at my spot I turned and looked for Mama and waved. Each time she waved back and laughed.

David fired the ball to the plate and they hit it and I watched as they scored twelve runs. The ball came out to me once and I ran to the fence and picked it up and threw toward where people were running and screaming. Finally everybody started running back to our dugout, so I went too. Fishook walked to the mound and slammed the ball to the catcher. Boom!

We ran back out to the outfield, where I waved at Mama and she laughed and waved back so I waved again and she waved again and then I heard the voice of my father from the dugout like it was right on top of me: "James!! Watch the ball! Play ball out there!"

They scored runs and one time a ball came my way and I threw down my Stan Musial glove and started running after it. I could really run fast when I put my head down. The ball bounced and bounced and I almost had it, but it bounced again and then it hit the fence. I picked it up and gave it to somebody. Finally, we got them out.

When we ran in to our dugout for the third inning, there was His voice again, growling, "Terry's up, Woody on deck, and little Rob'son in the hole. Get a bat and loosen up." He called me by my last name. My own father. Why? He said I would be third batter up to the plate. I did not plan to bat, but there was some misunderstanding about the situation. Apparently Daddy and the rest of the team thought I would go up to face Fishook. Nonsense.

The first batter was up in the third inning and it seemed like a perfectly good time for me to go to the bathroom. I walked down the third base side of the field and past the outfield fence and entered the cinder brick outhouse. I opened the stall door and closed it and locked it behind me. I looked down at the wooden toilet and held my breath against the stinky smells of the outdoor toilet in midsummer. There I remained, silent, alone, safe. They would forget all about me. After all, I was playing right field and batting ninth, which proved I was the least important player on the whole team. No one would even notice. I stood there and wished I was at home riding my bike down the hill with no hands, feeling the cool breeze on my face.

"James!" the deep gravelly voice of Zeus thundered through my dreams, "You in there?"

"Huh, yeah."

"What the hell are you doin'?"

"Pee-pee'in"

"Get out of there, you're up to bat!"

"I don't want to."

"James, come out of there right now. You're holding up the whole game."

I unlocked the stall door and walked out into the sun where Daddy stood holding a bat. He stuck the bat in my hand and we hurried up the path toward home plate. Everyone looked at me and waited as I walked toward the batter's box, alone, holding a bat.

Then I heard his voice again, this time in a different tone, a tone that I heard on rare occasions from him and a tone that I longed for. "James!"

I turned around.

He was walking toward me. "You scared, son?"

"Well, what does that hook thing do?"

He walked to where I stood and hunkered down on one knee. He put his arm around my shoulders and I could smell the familiar aroma of tobacco and his sweat-stained ball cap.

"Time out, Ump, he's a little nervous. I'll coach him a little."

We stood at home plate. "Now hold your bat just like this. And old Fishook is going to throw that ball. He throws a pretty good little curve ball. Now, he'll throw it up here and it'll be coming right at your head ..."

"It will?"

"Yeah, he'll throw it right up here. But, don't you duck!"

"Don't duck?"

"No, sir. See, that's what that hook is. He's got a dang good curve ball for a young fella. It'll look like it's gonna hit you but then it'll break right down over the plate. So, you have to hang in there and wait for it to break."

"Oh."

"All right, now, get up there and get set. And don't you duck."

Everyone was looking at me. The other team, our own team, all my friends, even the parents behind the backstop were looking at me and yelling at me. "You can do it James! Swing that bat!" "Pull the trigger now, little Rob'son." "Hang in there and take your cuts!" "Be a little man, now, and swing that bat."

Don't duck. That is the real secret. My Daddy told me.

Be a man. Face the monster. Don't be afraid. Charge up that hill. Into the valley of death rode the six hundred. Follow orders. Take your medicine. Do your job. Face the music.

Fishook wound up and fired the ball. I stood there in my tennis shoes and my little blue baseball cap and watched the white blur approach the plate and heard it hum as it buzzed through the air getting nearer and nearer, much quicker than I had thought possible. My Daddy was right. It was coming right at my head. But I had the secret message ... don't duck. The ball was spinning right beside my little blue baseball cap and I waited for it to perform this incredible feat of magic and suddenly curve downward over the plate for the strike and maybe I would swing and hit the ball. The faint smell of horsehide mingled with the hum of spinning threads inches from my head, and I waited for the ball to do what my Daddy said it would do.

Suddenly little stars appeared all over the ball field, sparkly lights of red, green, blue, lots of blues, flashed off and on and swirled together around my head. The air seemed to suck out of my lungs, leaving me without air to breathe. Loud bells rang in my head. My world turned upside down. The sky was below me and the green grass of the infield was above me. The umpire in a thick metal mask (to protect him from being hit in the head by Fishook's thrown ball) looked down at me from upside down. Birds seemed to be chirping by the hundreds in the nearby trees. From behind the black mask I heard him ask, "You okay?"

Do I look okay? Lying down here on the dirt looking up, wondering how I got down here, with a throbbing pain increasing steadily with each heartbeat? Does this look okay to you?

There was a low murmur of oooohhhs and aahhs from the stands. "Grady, for cryin' out loud—go check on him," Mama yelled to Daddy.

Something has gone wrong here.

My father looked down into my face.

"James, you okay, bud?"

"Uh-huh!"

Oh, sure. Just took my first real baseball pitch right in the head. Batting helmets had not been invented yet.

"Yeah, I'm okay."

"Atta boy! Get up now. Go to first!"

I got up. My head was pounding. The colors and outlines of objects like dugouts, trees, fences, and people seemed to blur and run together.

"Don't cry. Go to first."

I looked for Mama in the stands and walked a few steps toward the backstop where she was sitting. Then I saw her standing against the fence, looking at me sadly. "You okay, hon?"

"James!" the voice said. "First is over yonder. Hurry."

I must go to first base. But I am dizzy and can't seem to focus on a direction. Then I heard the voice say to the umpire as I stumbled toward first, "Wonder why he didn't duck?"

As I reread this version of the story I am again reminded of the tremendous differences between the written and oral versions. If I recorded and transcribed an oral version, it would be different in actual wording from the above, and yet, the overall effect would be similar. The oral version would be filled with incomplete sentences, "ya knows," vernacular, voice intonations, exaggerated pronunciations of words from my father (in his deep voice), the childlike voice of our little hero, the feminine voice of my mother, pauses, starts, and stops.

This story has been orally delivered to tens of thousands of listeners. It is a classic rite-of-passage tale with universal touchpoints. It is self-revelatory and plain old fun. The response to this by many people recalling their Little League experiences or their children's is powerful, touching, and, quite honestly, much more profound than I could ever have anticipated. From the simple origins of a childhood mishap emerged a story that is poignant and has the power to connect with even the most difficult audience.

Each of you has a personal Fishook in you: that pivotal moment with profound meaning. Locating it through self-reflection (and storyboarding) and basic story development puts you one step closer to your goal of using storytelling to become a stronger, more effective speaker.

# EXERCISE

## WRITING YOUR STORY

Writing out your story to place in a notebook or computer file is quite different from writing your story for publication as a short story or literature. Here we are only concerned with the outline and structure.

Step 1.  Choose one of the icons or symbols from your storyboard.

Step 2.  Formulate in your mind the Supreme Ordeal, the heart and soul of your story.

*The Supreme Ordeal.* A little boy goes up to bat to face Fishook—and his inner fears.

Step 3.  Find a beginning point, a separation or call to action.

"Jamesy, better find your ball glove, you're gonna be in the game tomorrow."

Step 4.  Now enjoy telling your story on paper. You have a crisis in mind, a beginning point. Go for it and have fun. The victory or wrap-up will reveal itself.

Step 5.  You now have a potentially powerful future signature story down on paper.

A.  You will rewrite, edit, embellish, fidget, and tweak. That's good.

B.  We'll discuss oral delivery later.

C.  Set the story aside for a few days.

Step 6.  Just in case this story does not evolve to the level of a keeper, I suggest you write out another story tomorrow, and the next day, and the next day, for one month. After one month you will have 30 or so first drafts of a scene, event, experience, or complete story. I can assure you as one who loves a good story that among your group of stories will be two, three, or even more potentially fabulous personal stories.

# 9 SIR GAWAIN MEETS FISHOOK

At a first reading or hearing of the story I call "Facing Fishook," we find an amusing childhood story. But upon further examination, there lies a deeper story—layers and layers of meaning, emotion, psychological crises, universal archetypes, and many allusions to universal myths.

In order to appreciate the parallels, we will look at the second half of "Facing Fishook" and see two life-altering issues that lurk beneath the surface.

When I tell the story to a live audience, I now include a second section of the story, usually after I have made practical applications and even gone on to a few other topics.

I segue back into the story by saying, "Sometime later I was seated at the end of the bench, hoping the game would be over soon so we could go to the Dairy Delight and get a chocolate malt with thick ice cream and malted milk. The other boys chattered and laughed, and David had even hit a ground ball and almost made it to first base. Mama suddenly appeared beside me on the bench, where I sulked and refused to talk or move. I put my head in her lap. She rubbed the sore knot on my head and I wanted to go to sleep in her arms. It was heaven.

Then a dark shadow moved over my feet.

"Wilma," the voice said, "we'd rather not have the mothers down here on the bench."

"Grady," she snapped, "I'm going to sit right here with this boy. Do you understand?"

"Yes, Ma'am!" he said.

But Daddy whispered something to her and she went back to her place in the stands. Then, the Voice thundered through my dreamlike, timeless place: "James! You're up, Hoss!"

Nowhere to run, nowhere to hide except within my own mind.

"James! Come on, son. Get back up there and take your cuts, Hoss. You can do it!"

The other boys looked at me. I looked at them and felt deeply shameful that I was afraid.

I walked back up to the plate and this time I was really scared. Fishook fired the ball. I stood frozen in place. The ball was coming right at me. I closed my eyes and put up my hands. The ball slammed into my side. Don't believe I could've taken two in the head that day ... (pause) ... I might have ended up President.

[My Arkansas roots have already been mentioned in the speech and President Clinton's well-known Arkansas heritage sets up this very funny line. Later we'll discuss humor, the context of humor, setups, knock-downs, and planned spontaneity.]

Don't cry and don't rub it. That's what everyone said. I stumbled to first, trying to suck some air back into my lungs, thinking how much fun it was to play baseball.

That is the end of the story itself. The following is the typical commentary that I might use to expound on the point of the story. During childhood and on into adolescence and even young adulthood, I played baseball. And every time I came up to bat I relived that first experience. Inside I was scared witless that I'd be hit by the pitch, but on the outside I attempted to act brave and be a man. I snorted and scratched and spit and acted like a real ball player. My inner fear was an embarrassment to me, and a source of shame. I felt less than a warrior, less than a man or a knight. As the years went by, my shame grew distant as adult issues invaded my life.

When I began to write stories about childhood events and later to tell them to live audiences, some of those childhood issues resurfaced. The event itself was of little importance to my teammates, my brother, my father, or my mother. Fishook doesn't remember it either.

## "SIR GAWAIN AND THE GREEN KNIGHT"

The Fishook story had evolved into its present form by 1992. During the spring of 1992—forty years after the event itself—I was enrolled in graduate studies in English literature. Seated in the school cafeteria at the University of Missouri at St. Louis, I was reading "Sir Gawain and the Green Knight." I began to cry. The other students probably wondered what the old guy was reading. I was not too surprised to find a clear-cut three-phase hero's adventure model within this popular Arthurian legend. What shocked me to my toes in Gawain's story was the dozens of parallel psychological touchpoints and uncanny similar archetypes found in "Facing Fishook"—my story, that had fully evolved long before I understood the word *archetype* or read the Gawain story.

Let's look at the story of Gawain. As I paraphrase the tale, I include some text as we move to a close (you must hear Gawain's exact words). You may wish to look for archetypes such as the Hero, a father or King, other knights, the monster or main enemy, the challenge or journey, weapons, a feminine helper, a crisis point, the Supreme Ordeal, a return, or a victory. Also, look for the emotional issue of facing fear and the subsequent shame of fear.

Here's a very brief overview of the tale.

King Arthur's knights are seated around the round table. A Green Giant rides up to the castle and challenges Arthur to a head-chopping contest. Winner takes all. Sir Gawain, a young knight who has not yet accomplished the feats of Lancelot or Parzival quickly volunteers to take the place of the King. The Green Giant gets off his horse and places his head on the block and Gawain chops it off. The Giant gets up, picks up his head, gets on his horse, and says, "I'll see you in one year when I chop off your head."

One year later, Gawain faces the Green Giant. We must note that during the year Gawain performed admirably as a knight, having some very interesting experiences in the castle of Sir Bercilak. The most interesting were his three encounters with Lady Bercilak, who kept showing up in his bed wearing nothing but a smile and tiny little see-through negligee. These encounters with the sizzling Lady Bercilak, an Aphrodite archetype, are in contrast to a later encounter with an old woman, a crone, the great goddess, a Hera archetype, who gives him a green sash to tie around him for protection.

Gawain faces the Giant, who stands waiting with the big ax. The story of Sir Gawain is the story of a young knight facing his fate: whatever has to be endured to become a real knight. Get up there and take your cuts. Be a little man. And, don't you duck!

The text reads:

The ax is raised above his head.
I shall grudge not the guerdon, grim though it may
prove;
Bestow but one stroke and I shall stand still,
And you may lay on as you like till the last of my
part be paid.
He proffered with good grace
His bare neck to the blade,
And feigned a cheerful face.
He scorned to seem afraid.

"He feigned a cheerful face."

We see two stories centuries apart, but we have one story emotionally. "My feet moved me closer and closer to the plate and there was a bat in my hand. I stood at the plate and took my stance, but I was not in my body." Fishook looked in for the signal. The Giant raised the ax. Back to the text:

Then the grim man in green gathers his strength,
Heaves high the heavy ax to hit him the blow,
With all the force in his frame he fetches it aloft
With a grimace as grim as he would grind him to
bits;
Had the blow he bestowed been as big as he threat-
ened,
A good knight and gallant had gone to his grave.

Fishook snorted, spat to the ground, wound up, and fired. The ball was coming right at my head. But I won't duck. I smelled horsehide and heard the hissing sound through the summer air. I knew it was my destiny to be the only kid in Little League history to be killed his first time up to bat. Don't duck, he said, so …

Now a slight twist in the story of Gawain:

> But Sir Gawain as the great ax glanced up aside
> As down it descended with death-dealing force,
> And his shoulders shrank a little from the sharp
> iron.

Gawain's "shoulders shrank," or he flinched.

In my story I was warned not to duck. Don't flinch. It's not manly. Flinching is an outward indication of weakness in the warrior.

In Sir Gawain's case, the flinch of the shoulders was all the Giant was looking for, and abruptly broke off the stroke of death. The ax buried into the wood block and Sir Gawain was surprised that his head was still attached to his body.

The Giant chides him for flinching. My teammates used to chide me for "stepping in the bucket," a common term for what kids who are afraid of the ball do when they move one leg away from the ball and toward the dugout.

> "You are not Sir Gawain the glorious," the green
> man said,
> "that never fell back on field in the face of foe,
> and now you flinch for fear, and have felt no
> harm;"

The Giant chides Gawain for being less than a true knight just as "society" or "culture," through various coaches and well-meaning parents, chide their children for performing below certain expected standards.

Gasping for air, with knifelike stabs of pain in my head, stars flying around me, trying to gulp in some oxygen, I walked to first base.

Ashamed and humiliated that I had been hit, the pain would fade away in time and would prove insignificant in comparison to the permanent imprint made that day on my psyche, my heart, and my soul. A rite of passage for certain, and an event gone awry.

But there are more parallels. Our two heroes go back up to bat and back down on the block. Gawain was also ashamed of his un-knight-like flinch, and immediately put his head back down on the block, similar to our little hero walking back up there to face Fishook the second time.

> Said Gawain, "Strike once more;
> I shall neither flinch nor flee.
> But if my head falls to the floor
> There is no mending me!"

I walked back up to that plate the second time for reasons far deeper and more complex than I'll ever know. And I walked back up to that plate thousands of times during the next 12 years of very serious baseball. I was invited to a try-out camp by the New York Mets in 1964, and in 1967 pitched in the semipro National Baseball Tournament in Wichita, Kansas. And each time I went up to bat, I was afraid of being hit by the ball, but the shame of the fear was far deeper than the fear itself. I felt less than a real knight. Just as the Giant chided Gawain for being afraid and said, "You are not Sir Gawain the glorious," I was not a real knight.

Being afraid of the pitched ball took on more ominous meaning symbolically, and I suspected that I was a coward in other areas of life. As these numerous parallels unfolded before me, I was totally astonished. But there is even more in these parallel stories, and it is increasingly astonishing.

The Giant tricked Gawain with the second fall of the ax. This time he purposely nicked Gawain's neck, saving his life but leaving a scar. The reason the Giant purposely nicked his neck? The Green Sash tied about his waist, given to him by the crone or old woman, the feminine power, known in mythology as Wisdom. Gawain was saved by Wisdom, just as I was "saved" or given solace by my mother. Gawain returned to King Arthur's Court, but because he had been scared he felt ashamed of his deed. And, like any real man or knight, he was embarrassed that his salvation was not his manly power of battle, but the green sash, Wisdom. This ancient legend shows that the hero sets forth to win a prize, meets many obstacles, including a sexual temptation; or meets a Giant, the destructive masculine carried to its extreme in the symbol of head chopping; and is saved by the green sash, Wisdom of the balance between masculine and feminine.

Gawain told of his year in pursuit of the Green Knight, a year filled with heroic deeds; but for deeper reasons only hinted at in the text, Gawain was deeply ashamed of his scar.

> "The nick on his neck he naked displayed
> That he got it in disgrace at the Green Knight's hands,
> alone.
> With rage in heart he speaks."

In my own personal journey I learned that I lived "with rage (anger) in my heart" because of childhood issues about my father that have never been resolved. How many people live with inner rage or anger over childhood issues that were brought on by attempting to become a warrior, a knight, a real man by masculine battles alone, and therefore rejecting the Wisdom that would have provided salvation?

Like Gawain we grieve alone:

> And grieves with man a groan;
> The blood burns in his cheeks
> For shame at what must be shown.

Arthur himself (Gawain's therapist) tried to console him, but to no avail. Inner psychological trauma is deeply embedded, and Gawain lived the rest of his life in shame. What is most interesting in the story is that Gawain performed bravely, wisely, and courageously in each of the challenges that came his way. But he was stuck on this one issue of the nick on his neck. I played American Legion, college, and semipro baseball and some remember me as a fireballing relief pitcher. Yet my primary memory of baseball was that one "nick" or scar: fear of the ball.

After reading the story of Sir Gawain in the cafeteria that rather memorable day, it dawned on me for the first time in 40 years that, for that little 8-year-old boy to walk back up to that plate the second time that day required deep courage, courage that is highly admirable in a child or in a knight. There was no reason for me to react to being hit with such a strong psychological trauma. But I did so, just like Gawain of old. Recently I spoke to the National Association of High School Athletic Directors, more than one thousand professional coaches, ADs, and teachers committed to making warriors, knights, and ball players of mere children. They were deeply moved as we peeled back layer upon layer of underlying meaning in this story.

I then took it a step further. Using the same story, I looked at the scene from my father's perspective. As a father and a veteran coach, he knew that it would be a terrible mistake if I sat beside my mother in the dugout and refused to go back up to bat and *try again.* He knew that life itself is about getting knocked down and getting back up and trying again. He was right. I'm an adult now, a grown man, and now I know that life itself is about facing a fastball everyday. The potential for lessons learned, values, and points to be made in stories is unlimited.

The partially true and partially embellished story I call "Facing Fishook" is filled with human psychology, emotion, and Divine Wisdom, just like "Sir Gawain and the Green Knight," Parzival and the Fisher King, *The Odyssey, Beowulf, Lonesome Dove,* and *Star Wars.*

Your stories, when developed and delivered properly, will contain within them all the power, insights, lessons, and challenges of the Great Story.

## Archetypes and Allusions

Let's list the parallel archetypes in the two stories. One is a childhood story apparently about Little League baseball but much more about an important rite-of-passage event with the three phases clearly seen; the other is an ancient Arthurian Legend about a young knight, but more so about a rite of passage with the three phases also clearly seen.

| *Sir Gawain* | *Sir Grady Jim* |
| --- | --- |
| 1. The Hero | The Hero |
| 2. Knights of the Round Table | The baseball team |
| 3. King Arthur | Father-coach |
| 4. Green Giant | Fishook |
| 5. Head chopping contest | Baseball game |
| 6. Ax | Ball |
| 7. Old woman (feminine wisdom) | Mother |
| 8. Green Sash (Symbol of salvation) | Hugs, sympathy |
| 9. First ax fall | First at-bat |
| 10. Gawain Flinches | Grady Jim hit |
| 11. Second ax fall | Second at-bat |
| 12. Nicked by ax | Hit by ball |

| | |
|---|---|
| 13. Saved by sash | Saved by wisdom/ Humor |
| 14. Shamed and angry within | Shamed and angry within (until the issue is resolved in adult life) |

The victory of my story is in the telling with humor these many years later. Each time it is told with humor, insights, lessons, challenges, and morals, a victory is won both for me and for every listener.

# EXERCISE

## A PERSONAL STORY WITH MYTHIC PHASES

It is difficult for me today to clearly separate the early development of "Facing Fishook" from later additions made when I was aware of the archetypes and mythic allusions. Some of my later additions were consciously made to experiment with archetypes, such as my father as both mentor and authority figure in the same person.

Even though some of the archetypes were purposely added, I continue to be amazed at the many parallels between "Sir Gawain" and "Facing Fishook."

This exercise will help you identify the 12 stages of "Facing Fishook," and later the phases in your own story. Refer back to the written version of "Facing Fishook." The 12 stages here are taken from Christopher Vogler's subphases.

| *Stage* | *Briefly describe the parallel stage in "Facing Fishook."* |
|---|---|
| 1. Ordinary world | _____ _____ |
| 2. Call to adventure | _____ _____ |
| 3. Refusal of the call | _____ _____ |
| 4. Meeting the mentor | _____ _____ |

5. Crossing the first
   threshold

   _____

   _____

6. Tests, allies, and enemies

   _____

   _____

7. Approach (to the
   Supreme Ordeal)

   _____

   _____

8. Supreme Ordeal

   _____

   _____

9. Reward

   _____

   _____

10. The road back

    _____

    _____

11. Resurrection

    _____

    _____

12. Return with elixir

    _____

    _____

You probably identified 10 of the 12 parallels very easily. Reward and the Road back are a bit vague. I am far more intrigued by the ten perfectly fitting phases. The three primary phases—call to adventure, crossing the first threshold, and return—are clearly seen in all quest stories. One or more detail can be less clear.

Now, pick out one of your best stories and identify the twelve stages.

*Stage*

*Briefly describe the parallel stage in* _____.
[your story]

1. Ordinary world

   _____
   _____

2. Call to adventure

   _____
   _____

3. Refusal of the call

   _____
   _____

4. Meeting the mentor

   _____
   _____

5. Crossing the first threshold

   _____
   _____

6. Tests, allies, and enemies

   _____
   _____

7. Approach (to the Supreme Ordeal)

   _____
   _____

8. Supreme Ordeal

   _____
   _____

9. Reward

   _____
   _____

10. The road back

    _____
    _____

11. Resurrection       _____

                                              _____

12. Return with elixir       _____

                                              _____

# DELIVERY

> *"My design here is not to teach the method which everyone should follow, but only to show in what manner I have endeavored to conduct my own."*
>
> —*Descartes*

# 10 FROM WRITTEN STORY TO ORAL DELIVERY

From the written version of the Fishook story, let's look now at the transition, or evolution, toward a final piece of oral story art through the process of oral delivery. Even though your written version may never be published or even read privately, it will be of great value in the development of your story from written to oral delivery. There are at least three important benefits from writing down your stories:

1. The story is formed into the essential three phases of the Hero's Journey. This, in itself, is reason enough to put pen to paper. The three phases give the story a skeletal structure that is set.

2. During the actual process of writing (and during later editing or rewriting) your subconscious will supply you with an abundance of delicious details. Sounds, smells, reconnections, bits of conversations, humor, pain, pathos, and other emotions rise to the surface. When I write a story from childhood, it is not unusual for me to be filled with deep emotions, remember-

ing my mother's love and support and my father's wit and humor, and I often close the story in tears. Those tears reflect the level of feelings the readers or listeners might experience. If a story does not have strong emotional impact for you, it will not have an impact on the listener.

3. The story becomes a separate piece. When we place that story in a computer file or manila folder, it takes on the form of a little piece of your life. Of the hundred or so stories I have written down, only about a dozen have made it to the stage, and fewer than that became signature stories.

## THE ORIGIN AND DEVELOPMENT OF "FACING FISHOOK"

By now, you should be an expert on the Fishook story. At the risk of overexposure, I must continue to use it as an example of personal story development and delivery by looking at differences between written and oral storytelling.

The origin of the story goes back to my son's first game of Little League baseball. His team was beaten soundly by the score of 68 to 5.

Somebody later asked, "Grady, didn't they have a ten-run rule after five innings?"

I said, "Yeah!" (The implication is, and the audience infers correctly, that the game was so one-sided that we didn't get to the fifth inning.)

Later, I learned to quip, "We didn't get to five innings. We started that game at 8 a.m. and broke for lunch in the top of the second inning."

It's almost impossible to discuss the process of written to oral development without some exploration of humor. Humor flows out of the in-the-moment development.

Development, humor, and delivery go hand in hand. When I told a few golf buddies about the score of the game, there was much laughter. After all, 68 to 5!

The written version is funny, but the live delivery is much funnier because of the facial expression, a look of incredulity: "Yeah, we didn't get to five innings." The timing is possible when I know the line is going to have them laughing. After the line is delivered, I use another professional comic trick, the raised eyebrow, that milks the laughter almost as long as you can hold the expression. Jack Benny was known for his stare at the audience with his hand flat against his cheek. Audiences who are really "in fun"—that imaginary bubble of new reality created by the speaker-comedian—will laugh as long as you let them. After the delivery of a solid laugh line, a simple raised eyebrow allows the audience to continue to participate with their laughter. You cannot learn this with written humor. It requires oral delivery. In discussions about humor, the idea of timing seems to be of great importance to everyone. It is important, but it is not as mysterious or difficult as it may appear. The teller of a tale should know exactly when laughter is expected from the audience and simply allow them to laugh. Only in oral development can that be learned.

Timing is built into the rhythm of the story. The silence or space between, "Yeah" ... (pause) *and* "... we didn't get to five innings" is timing and is learned in the process of presentation.

Although I had told the story of my son's game a few times, I had not yet thought of my own experience with Fishook as a good story. The actual reason for the lopsided score in my son's game was the pitching machine used that day to throw the ball. It was apparently geared to a very high speed, and the other team had been practicing against that speed, thus 68–5.

## CHAPTER TEN

The next week Ryan got out of the car, looked at the machine and said, "Dad, I don't believe I want to bat today!" Fishook of long ago immediately popped into my head. Within a few days I was telling the story of my son's game in my nightclub act, and soon entered Fishook.

Success in comedy clubs is measured in LPMs—Laughs Per Minute. Routines must have laugh lines almost back to back to back, or almost every line. Stories told from the professional speaker's platform generally do not carry that kind of humor. Therefore, in order to work well in a comedy club context, they must be edited or altered to eliminate non–laugh lines and to add laugh lines. "Facing Fishook" evolved over a period of about six months and perhaps as many as 50 oral tellings.

## HOW STORES ARE EDITED

The very first time I tell about an incident, an event, or a personal experience (sometimes privately to friends and sometimes to 500 people, being very aware of the context), it may very well be a one-laugh story. A story can evolve out of one funny line or incident.

Let's look at the growth process of a story other than "Facing Fishook," and see how a good story evolves out of one incident.

I was flying from Little Rock to Fort Smith, Arkansas and hurried to the counter of a small Arkansas airline. Here's what happened: "I walked up to the ticket counter and the woman looked at me and said, "Hon, how much do you weigh?"

A simple incident that I thought was amusing and unusual. Think about it—"How much do you weigh?" I didn't embellish or stretch the incident at the first telling. It's fair to do so but in this case I just reported the incident. Friends and family laughed at the line, at the thought of it; what a potentially weird scene. Now, watch the story grow in the hands of a class clown ...

*Second Telling:* "I walked up to the ticket counter in Little Rock and this gal is filing her nails and chewing gum. (Naturally I pretend to chew gum and file my nails.) 'Can I get on that flight to Fort Smith?' She didn't even look up. 'Hon, how much do you weigh?'"

*Third Telling:* "I walked up to the ticket counter in Little Rock and this gal is filing her nails and chewing gum. 'Can I get on that flight to Fort Smith?' She didn't even look up. 'Hon, how much do you weigh?' I said, 'What do you mean?' She said, 'Hon [I use my best southern waitress voice], we got a single-engine four-seater. I can weigh your bag but you've got to tell me how much you weigh.' [Addressing the audience, I say,] 'Well, I've been out of high school a long time, and I don't tell people how much I weigh.' So I lied! I get on this little single-engine four-seater. There is one other passenger, a woman. I don't do fat jokes, so let's just say she'd been out of high school awhile too! Or, as your mother would say, she's just a big-boned woman. We get strapped in and we start down that runway with the engine roaring. [At this point I hold my portable 'mike' very close and create a very realistic airplane engine sound, a funny sound, as the engine strains to get us airborne.] Then it hits me—I lied about my weight. Before I could say a word, the woman grabbed my arm and yelled, to me, 'Hon, if you lied like I did, we're gonna roll to Fort Smith!'"

Now I have a very funny opening story about Arkansas. The story closes on a huge laugh line. We've gone from a brief incident or scene to a 3-minute story with characters' voices, jokes, visual images, and more.

CHAPTER TEN

## HOW TO ADD AND ELIMINATE

Begin with an amusing or funny line. Add lines that work well but quickly eliminate lines that don't get a laugh. You have to eliminate or edit the scene down to a core bit. Now, find those good lines that work and add them to the story. All added laugh lines are, of course, memorized as you continue to tell the story. Pick and choose which lines you use in the moment. Here are some additional lines for my airplane story:

1. The airline was called Razorback Roulette Airways.
2. They don't sell tickets, they sell "chances."
3. She had the big hair, you know the kind; you'd recognize it if your girlfriend's hair has ever ruined a ceiling fan (Jeff Foxworthy).
4. The pilot was 14 years old.
5. After a long engine groan sound, I say, "We couldn't get the tail wheel up off the runway!"

A story begins not with a story, but with a funny scene or event, which is told and retold while you eliminate unnecessary nonlaugh lines and accidentally find new laugh lines. The first version may have been two minutes, and you remember the laugh of the listener. You tell it again, and this time you may not get a laugh where you thought you would. You may try it again, once or twice, but if it fails the next time, eliminate that line and move on. Tell the story again and edit it down to only the solid laugh lines.

When the story is cut down to its briefest form, with two or three laugh lines, you will have a very tight, dependable event evolving into a story. The story will then begin to grow in length as new laugh lines are found. The new lines often occur by accident, and sometimes by a friend offering a funny line about the story. From that point on, add only lines that get a laugh or set up a laugh line. For example, I have a line in "Facing Fishook" that I use in the oral telling but I don't even attempt in the written version. After I describe the awesome fastball of Fishook, I say, "The only kind of pitch I'd ever faced was my mother's in the backyard."

Funny? Maybe. But while I am saying the line I take on the role of my mother, and very graphically and cartoon-like, I pitch underhanded to the imaginary boy. Then I add (all in a motherly voice), "Here you go, hon! Hit the ball ... good try ... throw it back. Okay, hon, just roll it back."

The entire line was given to me by a very talented veteran comedian, St. Louisan Craig Hawksley. It was a funny idea that came to his mind as he recalled his own childhood. I put the line in the story the next time I told it, and it was instantly successful. The story grew and finally reached its full length within a year.

The story can grow with each live rendition. Speaker–audience chemistry creates energy within a context that invites exaggeration and embellishment. The story now increases in LPM's and, naturally, in length.

## "DON'T YOU DUCK!"

Why is a line funny? Will we ever really know? Maybe never to the full extent, but I'm convinced, after 25 years of attempting humor with my own stories, that the answer lies mostly in the delivery. Written humor can be wildly funny. Consider Dave Barry, S. J. Perelman, Woody Allen, Dan Jenkins, and George Carlin. But orally delivered, humor is a sizzling, in-the-moment human experience that is totally participatory and a group event.

Laughter is a shared event. When people in an audience laugh together, they are in an act of sharing, participating with others and the speaker. They are in a relationship that is very real and connecting. Listeners experience the source; it's almost a physical thing.

Comedians in clubs hear the material of their fellow comedians dozens and even hundreds of times. When a fellow comedian makes an effort to hear a particular bit or routine for the hundredth time, and then laughs heartily at that routine, you begin to see that the humor is not in the words themselves, but in the in-your-face delivery. They experience it again and again.

The Fishook story began to grow and fellow comedians would make sure they were in the doorway of the green room to see some of the action as our little hero approached the supreme ordeal.

## WRITTEN VS. ORAL DELIVERY

Here's the written version of the hero's attempt to bat, the words only:

"Now, get ready, stand right here. He's gonna throw that ball right at your head."

"He is?"

"Yep, he'll fire it right up here, but don't you duck!"

"Don't duck?"

"No, siree, it'll be spinning and that's why they call him Fishook. It will hook right down over the plate."

Allow me to explain through running commentary on the oral version. In the live presentation of this story, there is already a context. As always, the context is extremely important. The hero has already described his father the football coach, with his gravelly voice, big, and an authority figure.

His older brother is the star pitcher and cleanup hitter, and the audience is envisioning the scene within that context. All the archetypal allusions we saw in "Sir Gawain" are parading through the subconscious minds of every listener.

"He's gonna fire that ball right at your head." I say the words "right at your head," with an attitude. I know it's a good laugh line and therefore I say it with confidence, wait for the laugh, which we call timing, use the raised eyebrow, and milk it: "right at yoré head!" Yes, I exaggerate my father's southern-country twang.

"He is?" I change to my little-boy voice, with a look of confusion. This visual humor or look doubles the impact. The audience begins to sense what is coming. Anticipation is a big part of humor.

"But don't you duck!" This line is filled with meaning. The listeners now know the ball is going to come right at my head, and disaster is about to happen. Fathers think about their own fathers and sons. Mothers think about their daughters and sons in all kinds of roles.

"Don't duck?" Again, in confusion, the hero attempts to understand. I utter these words with more suspicion than earlier. He will go to bat for the authority figure. He will take the ax for his beloved leader.

"No, siree, he'll fire that ball right at your head, but it'll be spinning and will break right over the plate." This line is explanation to any audience member who may not know what a curveball is or fully understand at this point where we are in the story. If you are a careful reader, you will notice a slight difference between the wording just given and the same line in the written version that appeared in Chapter 8. I did that on purpose, to highlight the idea of free-word storytelling vs. memorization.

Let me explain. There are two schools of thought in regard to the memorization of your story as opposed to a kind of free-wording style. Legendary speaker Bill Gove is an advocate of memorizing every word in the story. Another platform legend, Bob Murphy, is equally committed to a free-wording style until the punch line, which is almost always delivered in exact wording.

Both styles work, although personally I lean toward the second style. I'm an advocate of memorizing only the essential laugh lines, and free wording the rest of the story. Some people find this impossible, but free-wording means you tell your story with a kind of first-time spontaneity even after 200 tellings. I've been accused of never giving the same speech twice. It's true. I have memorized only the lines that are essential to perfected humor.

"He's gonna fire that ball right at your head."

"He is?"

"Yep. But don't you duck!"

These lines are set in concrete; most other lines in the story are slightly different each time, but paint the same basic picture. I paint a picture with free wording that moves the hero into a position where I can use memorized and perfected graphic lines. By memorized, I do not mean the memorization of words only by reading off a script. Speakers do not memorize lines like actors on stage or screen. Speakers memorize certain words essential to the best humor; they do so through multiple tellings of the story. Furthermore, the facial expression, voice tone and volume, and effective body movement as well as positioning on stage are memorized. This is not perfected in practice or rehearsal, but from onstage, live telling as the story develops.

Storytelling is developed live, not on paper. "Don't you duck!" is a meaningful line. In this context, the authority figure's instructions are obviously absurd, so the audience anticipates what is about to happen. We see the awesome power of personal story to reframe an event and show that scene from the viewpoint of the hero. Story allows the storyteller to reveal depths of human experience that a listener may never have experienced in exactly that way.

The written version can be amusing and even funny. But the live or oral version is virtual reality, filled with sizzle, relived in front of the audience with all the flesh and bone and blood and sweat and smell of horsehide and sound of spinning ball of the actual event. From a memorable childhood event, to a written outline highlighting the three phases of the Hero's Quest, to oral delivery with in-the-moment sizzle, the journey of developing your story is a fun and worthwhile one. Now let's get serious about being funny.

# 11 HUMOR IS CONTEXT-DEPENDENT, OR, YOU JUST HAD TO BE THERE

Have you ever recounted what you thought was a very funny story to your coffee klatch or car pool, only to have your listeners respond with a weak, "Oh, that's really funny." When friends or family have to tell you your bit is funny instead of giving you a hearty laugh, you realize it is not funny to them. You then say, rather meekly, "Well, I guess you had to be there."

And it's true. Humor occurs in the moment and is not easily reconstructed. You do have to be there, for humor is heavily dependent upon the context.

Humor is not easy—it just looks that way when done well. I recall facing a very tough IBM audience many years ago. Using every trick in the book and a few spontaneous tricks, I finally won them over. Afterward, a young IBM employee said, "Boy, must be nice traveling around and telling a few stories for a living."

I made it look easy. It is not.

For many people, injecting humor is the most difficult part of public speaking and storytelling. Just as that mysterious and indescribable quality known as charisma can't be taught, it's difficult to teach someone to be funny.

Don't panic: Most people have the ability to be funny. Your style of humor may not be the kind of knee-slapping comedy that breaks up an audience, but that's not essential to get your message across. Perhaps your humor is more subtle, the type that makes the audience smile and ponder your comment, or shake their heads knowingly as they relate to a similar life experience.

On the other hand, don't be so sure you're not a true comedian. Most people love to tell humorous stories about their lives and can be very funny, given the right context. In my work as a storytelling workshop leader, I can recall more than one attendee saying, "Grady, I can't remember a good story, and I certainly can't get people to laugh at my personal stories." Then, less than an hour later during lunch, that same person is telling a hilarious story about something his or her spouse did that very morning.

You probably can tell a funny story, too. I've seen shy, normally introverted people suddenly explode onstage with a wildly funny story, then walk offstage and slip back into their normal reserved personalities. Strange as it may seem, in my earliest years as a speaker, I was convinced that my humor was confined to spontaneous ad libs. I didn't think I could write humorous speeches that would work in every situation. I was wrong.

If you are a speaker, you have the potential to raise your humor quotient several levels. By developing your own personal style, you can become a much more successful—and confident—public speaker.

Why do professional speakers (including myself) concern themselves so much with the use of humor? There are the obvious reasons: Humor is a natural icebreaker. You can deliver a point with humor. Humor is fun. All those are true. In addition, humor is an ideal way to create some common ground. Your willingness to attempt humor, whether you're a minister, politician, teacher, trainer, or corporate executive, sends a positive signal and can break down the natural boundaries between speaker and audience. But those are not the real reasons a professional speaker uses humor. The pro is in the business of speaking. There are a dozen ways to deliver information in a meeting. The professional speaker must create the kind of impact that will make the program memorable and generate more business as a speaker. The pro must include high entertainment value in the program, and humor is the primary ingredient.

## IS HUMOR ALWAYS APPROPRIATE?

As I stated earlier, I almost never say *always*. That's because every context is unique. The decision as to the appropriateness of humor must be made in the moment. One of the keys to successful speaking is gauging the dynamics of an event so that you can make this kind of determination.

There are a few very rare moments when humor may not be appropriate, for example, when the CEO is announcing a merger that will cost 5,000 jobs or a major catastrophe.

That said, I believe that humor is almost always a safe bet.

The right touch of humor can be appropriate for even the most solemn occasions. Here are three examples that come to mind:

1. With a twinkle in his eye, Pope John Paul II told a lighthearted anecdote on worldwide television when

addressing the youth service during a visit to St. Louis, Missouri.

2. During the impeachment trial of President Clinton, former Senator Dale Bumpers of Arkansas used appropriate humor that was well received by the U.S. Senate.

3. In the very sad and reverent funeral service for young Isaiah Shoels, who was killed by student gunmen in Littleton, Colorado, there were at least a dozen very appropriate uses of humor that brought lightheartedness, joy, and hope to the mourners and television audience alike.

Obviously, a successful speaker must avoid tasteless, offensive jokes. While some stand-up comedians are known for their x-rated material, public speakers are on the opposite end of the spectrum. As a speaker, preacher, sales trainer, teacher, or politician, your job is to use humor as a powerful tool to assist you in getting your message across.

We'll look now at the most crucial factor in the successful use of humor: the context.

## CONTEXT, CONTEXT, CONTEXT

You've heard that old line about the most important factors in the success of a business: "Location, location, location." Likewise, nothing is more critical to the success of humor than the context in which it is used. As a young comedian, this is the first lesson you learn. A funny line that worked last night might not work tonight. Why? Who knows. But it is a crucial lesson for speakers who attempt to use humor. Audiences respond in different ways to the very same material. The speaker learns to tread lightly and dance with the audience. If they want to laugh, you go with it. But if they fail to laugh at a line that you expected a response from, you adjust to that too. There is an old saying among those who use humor in speaking: "What do you do when they don't laugh?" Answer: "Pretend you were serious and be a motivational speaker." Even top comedians are often surprised when an audience fails to laugh at a proven line. The cliché, "But seriously, folks," attributed to Bob Hope, was invented for just such a moment. Johnny Carson built a career around lines that bombed in his TV monologue, coming right back with a funnier line about the bomb itself.

Humor is risky business, but by understanding the context and using developed stories in which you have total confidence, you can eliminate much of the risk. You can face a demanding audience and in a relaxed manner say, "Did I ever tell you about the time …?"

## SITUATIONAL HUMOR OR CONTEXT

Humor is context-dependent. Falstaff, Shakespeare's most memorable comedian from *Henry IV*, delivered lines that when read in script form seem unfunny and even cruel. But when acted out in the overall context of the play, his words are very, very funny. If the Sermon on the Mount had been delivered in bad lighting, with a faulty sound system and in a stuffy room, it is likely that Jesus himself would have received a lukewarm response.

Context is the most important factor in determining the success of a speech, especially with regard to humor. Here are two personal examples that illustrate this point:

*Place:* Missouri State Prison gymnasium.
*Audience:* Convicted felons in an obviously strained environment. The convicts were seated by their own

choice in a segregated manner, African-Americans on one side and caucasians on the other.

*Event:* Johnny Cash concert.

*Speaker:* Me. Here's how I was introduced: "Unfortunately, I am sorry to announce that Johnny had to cancel. In his place we have a comedian from Arkansas, Grady Jim Robinson." Can you imagine such a situation? Well, it really happened. When I walked out, I was greeted by raucous booing and catcalls. I sized up the situation, considered the context, and knew it was hopeless. And it was. I told my funny stories, and during the entire half-hour program (which felt like an eternity) there was not one laugh. I was escorted from the building under armed guard.

*Place:* Municipal Auditorium, San Francisco.

*Event:* Opening session at the Million Dollar Round Table.

*Audience:* Four thousand successful salespeople. (Accustomed to hearing America's best speakers, their expectations were extremely high.)

*Speaker:* Me. Introduced as one of America's top speakers, I rode onto the stage in a miniature cable car. I told the same stories that I had at the prison in Missouri, and received a standing ovation.

Was the material really that unfunny at the Missouri State Prison? Yes. Was the material really that funny in front of the prestigious Million Dollar Round Table? Yes. Same stories, same speaker—different context.

I'd like to think I can win over any audience at any given time and place, but it's just not true. That day at the prison, a disappointed, angry audience in a tense environment heard a guy tell a series of *Chicken Soup*-style stories. I was simply the wrong person in the wrong place. Richard Pryor, with his sizzling x-rated material about growing up on the rough streets of Peoria, would have killed (no pun intended) the prison audience that day, but by the same token he would have terribly offended the audience at the Million Dollar Round Table.

Politicians, teachers, trainers, preachers, CEOs, and banquet speakers must correctly assess the context and respond accordingly. The context can be accurately understood by taking into account the relational dynamics unique to each event, particularly four major factors: the audience, the event, the time and place, and the speaker.

## The Audience

I admit that my experience at the prison is an extreme example of an unreceptive audience. Most speakers can make it through their entire careers without facing such an extremely disappointed and unreceptive crowd.

In the two extreme examples given, there is a hidden current within the audience. That is expectation. I believe that the audience has a preconceived notion of what to expect and why they are there. Of all the possible relational dynamics, audience expectation is of crucial importance.

Every audience has expectations. They are in attendance for one or more reasons. I believe it can be said that every person in the audience is there to gain something, unless it's an auditorium full of kids attending a mandatory chapel service (which creates a whole new set of challenges). Most are volunteering an hour of their time to listen to a speaker because they expect to get something in return.

Look at four examples of audience makeup and what they might expect:

1. Schoolteachers, administration, and staff gather for in-service training the day before school begins. The teachers are looking for inspiration to take into a new school year, and perhaps some insights that may help them understand today's youth.

2. Lumbermen attend a two-day safety program that provides the latest techniques that will help them do a dangerous job more safely.

3. Insurance salespeople come to a convention to be motivated, to be educated on the latest laws, to learn about new products, to see old friends and colleagues, and to compare notes.

4. A Chamber of Commerce gathers for a banquet to install the new president in a community where most audience members know each other and have optimistic expectations for a new year.

Slight differences in expectation play a part in the speaker's approach.

## Mars and Venus Together

Most veteran speakers will tell you there is a big difference in audience response to humor depending on the gender mix. It may seem far-fetched, but this contextual dynamic is of primary importance.

An all-male audience is generally less responsive than an all-female audience. Men seem to have a natural resistance toward other males (including speakers) who presume to know something they don't. Humor is a critical factor in breaking down that resistance and assuring the male audience that you are not there as competition.

The type of humor men respond to is significantly different from the humor most enjoyed by women. Men tend to laugh *at,* while women are more prone to laugh *with*—an extension of basic gender psychology that might be overly simplified as competition (male) versus cooperation (female). An all-female audience is generally open and receptive. If the speaker is a woman, their expectations are slightly different than for a male speaker. As a southerner with a distinctive twang in my voice, I must quickly overcome the stereotypical assumption that I am a male chauvinist. Self-deprecating humor is an excellent way of letting women know I am not a chauvinist. Right away I usually mention a title of one of my speeches, "Women Are from Venus and Men Are Lost in Space ... and Won't Stop to Ask for Directions." This is a funny line that lets them know that I'm a sensitive modern male.

I find that the best audience is one that's evenly balanced between men and women. Men tend to soften up and become more receptive when women are present. Somehow, the presence of women reduces their natural tendency toward standoffish competition with another male. A female speaker addressing an all-male audience faces a slightly different challenge, especially if she is physically attractive. While we'd all like to think otherwise, it is difficult for some men to initially look past a woman's physical appearance. Injecting humor about that very issue goes a long way in allowing the men to relax and view the female speaker as a colleague.

### Laughter Is a Shared Experience

I always want to know the size of the audience. It is much easier to generate laughter and fun with a large crowd than with a small crowd. We don't have to understand fully why that is, but it just is. Comedians dread those late-night spots when the audience dwindles down to half a dozen people. The material that succeeds with a large crowd often falls flat with a small, tired group. The smaller the audience, the less energy will be created in a room. It's very difficult to make a group of 12 people laugh, but with a throng of 1,200 it's relatively easy to produce a ripple effect, because laughter generates more laughter.

The speaker should be aware of audience expectations, gender mix, and size.

## The Event

Although the audience and event are obviously interrelated, the event itself can be considered separately from audience expectations. The event may have a history, like the Academy Awards. Oscar night is so universally known in our culture that when the host is introduced, he or she faces a very knowing, expectant audience. The host is aware that he or she is involved in a cultural ritual in which the audience has very high expectations, yet will be very supportive if certain rules are observed. Billy Crystal and Whoopi Goldberg have interpreted the context and delivered accordingly. But what if I walked out as host of the Academy Awards and faced an audience that had no clue who I was? The dynamics would be different. (Naturally, I would tell a series of very funny stories that would win them over and make me rich and famous, and I would live happily ever after.)

The speaker must understand the nature of the event and plan accordingly. Here are two examples:

While jogging through the Washington Mall recently, I stopped at the Lincoln Memorial, where the words of the Gettysburg Address and Lincoln's second inaugural speech are engraved on the inside wall. Lincoln was a master speaker; but more than that, he totally understood the events at which he spoke so eloquently. He wrote the Gettysburg Address on the back of an envelope while on the train to

Gettysburg. He spoke for only a few moments that day and his speech was described in the papers the next day as rather dull. Lincoln was known for his humor, sarcasm, wit, and wisdom, but on this day he chose to speak solemnly and without humor. The event was the dedication of the Gettysburg Cemetery, where 30,000 young American men had died in a horrendous hand-to-hand battle. He correctly understood the event, and his simple address lives in American history as one of the most meaningful speeches of all time.

Lincoln's second inaugural address is not as well-known, but has an equally awesome impact upon the reader who today understands the historical context of his words in the midst of a civil war. His basic message that day, couched in formal language, was "We pray to the same God. Why are we doing this to each other?"

Understand the event itself. A Rotary Club meeting, a convention, a sales meeting, a Chamber banquet, an awards banquet: Each has a slightly different relational context.

---

### Helpful Hints for Prespeech Evaluation

I want to know as much as possible about the context surrounding a scheduled speech. By phone I interview the contact person and ask about the audience, the event, the time and place, and the context. Here's what I ask:

1. Who is the audience? How many are attending? Is it professional or industry? What's the age range? Gender makeup? Level of education? What are their expectations?

2. What is the event? Is it an annual event? Did the same audience attend the event the previous year?

---

> Who has spoken to this audience or event in the past? Are they accustomed to humor at this event?
>
> 3. What is the time and place? What programs are scheduled before the event? After the event? At what point in the program will I be introduced? Who will introduce me? How is the room set up? Is there a stage, platform, riser, head table? What is the audience seating: theater style, classroom layout, or round tables in banquet style?
>
> 4. Are there any highly controversial issues I should be aware of? Are there any mergers, downsizing, or in-house scandals I should know about?

## The Time and Place

The time of day during which you make a speech will often have a major impact on how it's received. Similarly, the place where you're speaking can play a crucial role in determining success or failure. I have appeared in almost every conceivable setting, from motel atriums with swimming pools and waterfalls to fabulous auditoriums with perfect sound systems; from hotel banquet rooms with no lighting whatsoever to golf pro shops where golfers in spikes clacked right through the audience, carrying their golf bags.

Here are some things to remember about time:

- An opening kickoff event at 9 a.m. is much better than a closing session at 4 p.m.

- A postlunch speech is usually a better time slot than just before lunch.

- One of the most difficult times to speak is around 2 p.m. after a long lunch program.

- The least preferred time for a speech is 4 p.m.

- A banquet event is usually a good time for a humorous, story-filled speech, assuming the audience has enjoyed a cocktail or two and you're introduced on schedule after a good dinner. However, a time slot at the end of a banquet that includes a two-hour cocktail hour, a seven-course meal, a star-studded program with a harpist, a glee club, a barber shop quartet, and 24 separate awards, is not a good context for a speech.

I once spoke at Disneyworld at 11:30 a.m. to a huge audience, with the children sitting in the front rows knowing that the only thing between them and Mickey Mouse was me. Not a good time.

Remember: While you can't set the time of your speech, you can be aware of the time and plan accordingly.

I have spoken to groups on the beach with surf pounding, under a full moon as listeners swatted at buzzing mosquitoes, in a California desert with fans roaring, in a golf pro shop, and in dozens of unlikely places too numerous to mention.

An inexperienced meeting planner is often unaware of the importance of the physical place in the success of a program. Speakers are often asked to speak in situations, times and places, or contexts that make it almost impossible to speak effectively. In such a setting, I can only hope for a good sound system and microphone.

### Change the Context

What can a speaker do who arrives on site, surveys the physical place for the program, and realizes the situation will be difficult?

1. *Your location in the room:* Without offending the meeting coordinator, you must take charge. As the speaker, you must decide where in the room is the best location for you to speak. Consider the sight lines of all audience members. Pay special attention to sight lines of those in the back rows.

2. *Seating arrangements:* Hotel workers are unaware of the role of room dynamics for the speaker. Make sure the front row of chairs is at the proper distance from the podium. If there are more chairs than people, it's far better to have people seated up front. (Note that during in-service training days in high school auditoriums, the audiences almost always fill the back rows first, leaving rows of empty seats up front. Try to move them forward. Better still, grab that handheld wireless mike, jump off the stage, and walk up the middle aisle to speak. This rather radical move creates an instant relational dynamic of energy in the room. The amateur speakers have remained behind the podium, delivering their nervous lines in a mechanical and rigid manner. Their discomfort is communicated instantly through body language and platform mechanics. That's why it is extremely effective for a speaker to take the mike, leap from the stage down to the floor, walk halfway up the aisle, and come face to face with the audience. Add the technique of opening with a strong story, "Did I ever tell you about the time ...?" and you're off and running.)

3. *Background:* Background is important. Although it is true that the speaker is at the mercy of whatever circumstances he or she is given, do your best to control the background.

4.  *Distracting outside sounds:* Nothing is more challenging than a wedding band blaring away in the meeting room next door. You may have little control over the sound throbbing through the walls. Hold that handheld mike even closer and talk louder ... and faster.

## The Speaker

Even if you have developed powerful stories, filled with well-timed, good humor, the context itself may be the most important factor. A talented, experienced, well-prepared speaker can end up in the wrong context. Because humor is context-dependent, the wise speaker will carefully consider the relational dynamics between the audience, the event, and the time and place. My most recent speech was in my hometown of Greenwood, Arkansas, where my stories originated. Many of the people in the audience knew my father, mother, brother, and sister. They had also read my stories about growing up in Greenwood in *Sports Illustrated* and *Reader's Digest* over a period of 20 years. The context was the traditional "hometown boy goes out into the world and then returns." In that context I, as the speaker, could hardly go wrong.

## HOW TO PREREAD THE CONTEXT

Consider the following examples of context. Think about the relational dynamics. In each example of a speaking event of mine, I'll highlight the basic context and then give a brief summary of how I preread the situation.

1.  *Audience:* Two thousand members of Toastmasters International.

    *Event:* Toastmasters International annual convention in Las Vegas. Their expectations are high in anticipation of a great convention. The opening keynote speaker is traditionally entertaining and provides an example of the platform skills each of them hopes to attain.

*Time:* 9:00 a.m. The Opening General Session.

*Place:* Main Ballroom, Bally's Hotel Casino.

*Sound:* Perfect sound system with handheld wireless mike.

*Lighting:* House lights up but not bright. Stage area well-lit.

*Seating:* Theater-style seating with aisles on the left and right.

*Context:* Most audience members were not familiar with me. They had read my biographical material in their programs and were slightly familiar with my background as a minister, comedian, writer, and second son of a high school football coach. They were aware that only experienced speakers are placed in these slots, so they were anticipating an entertaining and informative program. When all these components are considered, it is easy to see that the context is totally positive. This is a context in which any speaker can thrive.

Now, compare the above to another program.

2. *Audience:* Twelve salespeople, one boss.

*Event:* Sales training. First-time meeting for the group.

*Time:* 8:30 a.m.–12 noon

*Place:* A small meeting room, seated around a table.

*Sound:* No microphone.

*Context:* The twelve people were very disconnected from the event itself and seemed to resent being present. They had arrived the night before, two hours late, and while seated in the lobby a comedian performed while they ate appetizers. This whole atmosphere, which is another word for context, included many negative factors and made it very difficult to create positive chemistry within the group.

3. *Audience:* Five hundred salespeople. (I'm referring to the incident related in Chapter 2.)

   *Event:* Evening banquet for awards ceremonies, which included annual bonus checks. Their primary focus was on their own checks and how they might compare with the other guy's.

   *Time:* 5:30–7:30 cocktail hour, after a golf tournament including a hardworking beer wagon.

   7:30 Dinner

   8:30 Awards

   9:00 Speaker

   *Place:* Hyatt Airport, Dallas, Texas

   *Sound:* Good

   *Seating:* Round table with huge stage.

   *Context:* After a surprise appearance by the Dallas Cowboy Cheerleaders, I was introduced as Grady Bob Johnson. This context is fraught with difficulties. It could have gone either way. The audience is a high-energy crowd, slightly intoxicated, in high expectation of entertainment. Too much alcohol is a negative factor and one that many top speakers bend over backward to avoid. Humor is a primary tool for controlling such a situation.

## CHAPTER ELEVEN

The experienced speaker intuits the relational dynamics of every situation. Audience, event, time and place, and speaker are the four primary factors that must be fully understood for a speaker to be successful.

Humor is context-dependent, and the wise speaker will carefully consider the relational dynamics between the audience, the event, and the time and place in preparing appropriate humor. From the Academy Awards to the local Rotary Club dinner, from a deeply meaningful funeral service watched by an entire nation to the well of the Senate during a presidential impeachment proceeding, the speaker must correctly assess the context.

# 12 WHERE HUMOR REALLY COMES FROM

"Life is crazy and meaningful at once. And when we do not laugh about the one aspect and speculate over the other, life is exceedingly drab."

—C. G. Jung

"James, you were the happiest kid I ever knew."

—Sharon Percy-Blythe
(At Our Twentieth High School Reunion)

I am not an authority on humor. However, I am the world's leading authority on *my* humor. My first recollections of being funny, or funnier than most kids, go back to the sixth grade, exactly one year after my first experiences of failure, struggle, receiving terrible grades on report cards, and wondering what must be wrong with me. Some of my stories refer to bad grades in the second grade. In reality my grades were fairly average in the early grades, although other events, like being placed in the Canary reading group, occurred in the second grade. In the fifth grade, after a great fourth-grade year with Mrs. Craig as my teacher, I was placed in the room of a teacher who will remain nameless. My mother was the other fifth-grade teacher and I was dying to be in my mother's class. In those days even my supportive mother thought it best that I not be in her class. A big mistake. I hated my fifth-grade teacher and apparently she hated me. It was a traumatic year and I was a miserable child. It was during that year that I developed feelings of shame and guilt about being less than a prize student. The trauma was mostly in my own mind, and it may even be that I seemed like a happy kid. But on the inside things were falling apart.

In the sixth grade I became the class clown. As I write these words, my fourth-grade and sixth-grade report cards are lying before me. The fourth-grade report card reveals a happy and accomplished little student with a mixture of B's, C's, and even a few A's from Mrs. Craig ... my mother's best friend.

After the horrible and, I believe, life-changing fifth-grade year, my sixth-grade report card shows F's, D's, and a few C's, and something quite interesting: an A in reading. There is a handwritten note from Mrs. Shields, the teacher, to my mother: "Wilma, he is reading quite well now. I don't understand why he can't get the rest of his work?"

Our future comedian, storyteller, and lifelong reader and writer performs poorly in the primary competitive arena of his childhood grades in school. Later he writes stories about experiencing feelings of inferiority in sports competition. Forty years later my therapist would say, "Grady Jim, it appears you have a serious problem with head-on competition."

In the seventh grade, things got even worse. From childhood and elementary school to what is perceived as young adulthood, junior high school, I quickly went berserk. Junior high school was the pits. My attention span was nonexistent.

I could not focus on classwork and the need to know the eight parts of speech took on the weight of anvil around my neck. My grades got worse. Today I suspect that I would be diagnosed with ADD, but in those days a bad performer was a kid with "ants in his pants," or worse, an incorrigible smart-aleck or, to place a more positive spin on it, class clown. My lack of ability to focus in class led to deep frustration and failures.

Meanwhile, my brother David had become the star on the baseball, basketball, and football teams as well as a drummer in the Jazz Katz rock and roll band. He made A's and was considered handsome and the perfect boy. I was proud of Dave. But having a brother one year older who was outstanding in all areas of traditional competition placed even more pressure on me to succeed. In many of my early stories, the sibling rivalry theme was obvious. I was trying to compete with David in sports, music, academics, fishing, bike riding, and Boy Scouts.

It would be several years before the words of Frank Sulloway's *Born to Rebel* would help me see just how important the issue was. Finding head-on competition with an accomplished older brother impossible, I compensated by making humor out of the situation. My response was not unusual. Recent research shows that males in contemporary culture are forced to measure their self-worth in terms of masculine competition, usually in sports or other accepted masculine roles: cars, hunting, gangs, and so on. For a serious study of the influence of masculine competition on feelings of self-worth, I recommend Terrance Real's book, *I Don't Want to Talk About It.*

We move on in search of the true sources of humor.

Let's see now … basketball, baseball, football, and the Jazz Katz. Is anyone surprised that I later developed stories in which the little hero attempts to find stardom and success in those very arenas? My attempt to play football led to one of my first published stories, called "The Day I Tackled Billy Bob."

Obviously, "Facing Fishook" is my subconscious response to failure in baseball. And my first attempt to play basketball in high school, because my father insisted I play in a game, led to "Pine Tar," the story we will look at in this chapter.

Dave's success as the drummer in the locally popular rock and roll band, the Jazz Katz (they played in Fort Smith and Milltown, Arkansas and at most school assemblies) led to my one performance with the Jazz Kittens—and possibly the most hilarious school assembly in GHS history. I was the drummer. Unfortunate choice for the other boys, since I had never beat a drum in my life.

Bad grades, an overly sensitive fear and dread relationship with my father, suspicions that I might be a sissy in football, growing sexual energy creating self-loathing and shame, displacement in my own home in strange ways that no one could understand: It was during those three or four years of hypersensitive adolescent emotions, fears, hopes, and lost hopes that I became more and more hilarious, outrageous, rebellious, insecure, and frightened.

Most of my stories have their origin in elementary and junior high school. These were the least funny years of my whole life. Yet most of my stories come from those years of pain.

## THE ROOTS OF HUMOR

Funny stories recounted later in life about childhood events are almost always only half of the story, the funny half. That's why I was so shocked when Sharon Percy-Blythe said to me at our 20-year reunion, "James, you were the happiest kid I ever knew." My external self became more and more the show-off, the class clown, and from the outside I must have appeared the most happy-go-lucky kid in town. And I was happy. But I was also deeply troubled about certain issues in my life. "Life is crazy," said Carl Jung, "and meaningful all at once. And when we do not laugh about the one aspect and speculate over the other, life is exceedingly drab." I have laughed over its craziness and speculated, as a minister and a mystic, over the more serious side.

My choice, and it was a choice that I made, to become a comedian even in those times of personal pain, saved my sanity and my life. Looking back now, I see true humor in many of those events. Removed by time and space, the storyteller can either suppress the pain or use it as fuel for a form of self-expression. I chose to use my inner fear and confusion as fuel for showing off.

Richard Pryor broke new ground in comedy material by facing his childhood pain. His life as a child in Peoria, Illinois is deeply disturbing to read about in his autobiography. He was raised by prostitutes who were coworkers of his mother; terribly abused by his mother's regular customers, he survived on the streets through his adaptability, courage, and extraordinary sense of humor. Pryor lived a true horror story. He dared to address all those issues in his comedy art, which is terribly funny and disturbing.

Frank McCourt endured childhood horrors in Ireland far beyond what most Americans can grasp. At the age of 62 he wrote *Angela's Ashes,* filled with stories about his childhood trauma growing up the poor child of an alcoholic father. His book won a Pulitzer Prize.

James Joyce wrote *Portrait of an Artist as a Young Man,* ranked third by the Modern Library among the greatest books in the English language. The story of Joyce's childhood sounds strangely familiar: serious issues about his father; his failures in school regarding grades; trauma caused by his miserable failures in sports competition; and his growing sense of shame and guilt about sex in relationship to religious instruction.

Richard Pryor, Frank McCourt, and James Joyce created pure art with rich humor out of basic childhood trauma. Their childhood experiences were far, far more dramatic than my own. My childhood, compared to Pryor's, McCourt's, and Joyce's, could be viewed as very plain, normal, or even ideal. As the son of a popular coach and school-teacher, I enjoyed a childhood filled with bike riding, baseball, and the old swimming hole. That may seem like the perfect setting for a childhood, but the underlying currents and personal challenges of any childhood can be powerful and life-shaping.

The creation of personal story flows out of a backdrop of a lifetime. A theme emerges for each individual. My theme set a tone for the creation and development my own series of stories: a hero attempts to win approval in a variety of ways, is foiled again and again in the attempt, and learns and grows in the attempt—the classic Hero's Journey.

## EXAGGERATION AND EMBELLISHMENT

As a young adult I began to write about my childhood, apparently in search of some kind of completion. With an inclination toward humor, the stories seemed to beg for exaggeration and embellishment. The task became bigger than life, the foe became a huge monster, the Supreme Ordeal became even more supreme and more of an ordeal.

Is it fair to exaggerate the story? When discussing story development, this question is often asked. Some are reluctant to make up, embellish, and stretch the truth. There are those who feel their stories must be strictly historical truth. I fear this would lead to some very boring stories for most people. Reality is far more bland than we like to admit. Reflecting back upon an event allows us to recreate the event and purposely bring out aspects of the story that make it entertaining and worth telling. Storytelling is about stretching the boundaries and creating a story that transcends daily life and mere facts. We're not talking about testifying in a court of law here; we're talking about telling funny stories. If a storyteller has serious hang-ups about embellishment or creation of characters and scenes for the recreation of an event, I recommend that person seek a career in accounting.

The intention of the storyteller is as important as the expectations of the audience. When a speaker tells a funny story, there is a suspension of normal rules such that the audience is prepared to accept an outrageous exaggeration. The storyteller is expected to embellish the story. That's the whole point!

## RECOUNTING AN EVENT AS IT HAPPENED

Embellishment is accepted and encouraged but it isn't always necessary. Let's look at one of my popular stories that is the recounting of an event as it happened. This event was truly an embarrassment to me at the time it occurred, and I didn't think about this scene for 30 years. However, when I first told the story to 2,000 professional speakers, I relived the story as I remembered it. In other words, I recounted the story from within my own mind and therefore my own experience of embarrassment. It made quite an impression.

Unlike "Facing Fishook," which is highly fictionalized, "Pine Tar" happened just about the way I tell it. Fishook originated as a true event, being hit on the head in my first two Little League at bats. My father was the coach. My brother David was the pitcher. It was traumatic. However, the details grew out of a composite of many, many experiences with my father, my brother in his superior role, my mother rescuing me, and my inner feelings about it. The story has been fully embellished over years of storytelling—a little bit at a time.

In contrast to "Facing Fishook," which is a composite of many scenes, "Pine Tar" is a real event that needs little embellishment.

## "PINE TAR"

I was about to attempt my first pregame dunk, self-consciously tugging at my too-tight basketball shorts when the ball bounced toward me. The real trick was to get a tight enough grip on the basketball to go up and slam the ball downward through the hoop. I gripped and regripped. It was time to go for it. My first pregame dunk attempt was frightening enough, but it was my strange self-consciousness about wearing shorts in public that made that night one of the most memorable nights of my life.

An early crowd of a half-dozen parents and some junior high kids had arrived for the B game against Waldron, Arkansas, and they were surprised to see me out there in white shorts, shooting layups. I had steadfastly refused to play basketball, even though I was 6 feet, 3 inches tall.

Everyone assumed my reluctance to play basketball was because David was a star player as a senior, and I was afraid to compete with my older sibling. It's true, he was better than me in all sports; but fear of competing against Big Dave was not the reason I refused to play basketball. The truth was something far more complex and inexplicable: some quirk of immature boyhood had left me neurotically self-conscious about my legs, and even more so about my upper body.

In those days, the little undershirt-like jerseys the boys wore exposed to the world bony shoulders and skinny arms. And, unlike today's baggy knee-length trunks, the shorts worn were tight, with cute little pleats up the side.

So, there I stood, tugging at the too-tight shorts, and trying to grip the basketball for the pregame dunk my brother David had made a tradition at Greenwood High School.

My sudden appearance on the gym floor happened so fast, I had little time to even think about being self-conscious about my half-nakedness in front of the whole world. I had innocently wandered into the locker room before the game like I always did, as equipment manager of the team, which allowed me to ride the bus on all the road trips.

As I walked through the door, my father said in his deep, gravelly voice, while smoking his Prince Albert roll-your-own, "James, come here, bud."

"What's up, Pop?"

"We got a B game tonight, and we don't have but four players."

"So?"

"You're gonna have to play!" he said, digging in a box.

"Daddy," I said with horror, "I don't play basketball!"

He ignored my remark and tossed me a pair of satin shorts that were not even like the game trunks the other team members wore. "Here you go, James. You've got to play tonight. Just got four boys."

I knew my father had been watching out the kitchen window while David and I went one-on-one in customary blue jeans on the dirt outdoor court. Big Dave usually got the upper hand, but he was already all-district.

The satin shorts landed in my hands.

"Daddy, I don't play basketball," I pleaded.

Coach Grady Sr. was 6 feet, 6 inches tall and weighed about 260. He found it difficult to express his tender feelings to his own sons. I was surprised—pleasantly surprised—when he said in a distinct tone of tenderness, support, and perhaps some confusion, "Son, I don't know why you don't want to play. But I think you will do real good. Why don't you try?"

I dared not tell the real truth about some silly, self-conscious personal thing about exposing my legs and arms in public. It seemed so wimpy. There were no words to say. I just stood there and shuffled my big feet.

Slightly encouraged by my silence, he tossed me a jersey. "Here you go," he said excitedly, "I found this old undershirt left over from PE class. I put a number zero on it. You'll be number zero." He was a funny guy.

In every boy's life there are decisive, life-shaping moments. At such moments, it's not about winning the race, it's about getting in the race and trying. All that is required for the hero or heroine to embark on a life-changing journey is to say "yes" to the call.

I looked at the satin shorts and the ragged undershirt with the number zero scribbled in magic marker. There was no one else in the locker room. I heard the bounce of basketballs on the gym floor as the four other B teamers shot layups. My father's gaze was a look of hope for his second son, imploring with his eyes to attempt to break through to a new place.

"Okay," I said.

So. There I stood. Trying to get a good grip on the ball, wearing satin shorts that were way too tight, my number zero undershirt, borrowed tennis shoes, and black and pink argyle socks, looking like a combination of Ichabod Crane and Howdy Doody.

The pregame dunking tradition began when David became the first dunker in Greenwood history. Dave had an ingredient that enabled him to slam dunk in pregame warmup. A sticky magic potion ... pine tar, a greenish-brown, incredibly sticky, gooey substance. David set the jar of pine tar on the bench, dabbed a bit of sticky stuff on his fingers, drove in for a layup, went high in the air, and *boom!* Behold, the dawn of the dunk at Greenwood High School.

I dipped into the pine tar. It was time for me to try it. I bounced the ball once, regripped the ball, took three or four steps, and leaped upward. Never having experienced an adrenaline rush on the basketball court, I had no idea what would happen. Suddenly, I found my hand high above the rim and slammed a vicious dunk with the help of the pine tar. Naturally, I had to try it again and again, and, okay, one more time, each time with more pine tar. Unfortunately, that was the highlight of the night.

So, nervous, self-conscious, and disoriented my first time in a real game, I had trouble remembering which goal was ours. They both looked alike. Up and down the court we went, a blur of Greenwood blue, Waldron orange, and me in the white satin outfit. I seldom touched the ball as I followed my teammates up and down the floor, desperately trying to act casual and feeling very aware of my exposed arms and shoulders. The shorts were too tight, especially with my Jockey shorts underneath, and I was constantly reaching down and making a slight adjustment. After every movement, I would turn away from the crowd and sort of pull the shorts away from the crotch area, where things seemed to bunch up.

Halfway through the first quarter, I noticed one of my teammates, and then another, glancing down at the area at which I had been nervously tugging. Then it hit me ... the brown pine tar was still on my fingers.

The audience response to this line is usually a mixture of groans and laughter. It reminds everyone of their own embarrassing moments. I quickly tell the rest of the story: The next day I tried out for the basketball team, having endured the most painfully embarrassing scene possible for a kid overly concerned about his exposed body. I played basketball that year and the next, attended college on a basketball scholarship, and later played semipro. Now when I tell this story, I flash a picture on the screen of me dunking a basketball in my high school uniform. Victory.

Humor flows out of the reality of one's life experience. The humorist is one who has decided to turn life's trauma and everyday failures into humor in order to survive. The clown has a made a decision to view his or her failures as funny and therefore achieve a kind of victory out of the jaws of defeat.

Such stories as "Pine Tar"—and I'm convinced that every human being has a number of rite-of-passage childhood memories—portray common and universal childhood passages that form a young person's view of the world and his or her role in it.

My humor—maybe not yours, or Jack Benny's, or Robin Williams', or Jim Carrey's—was my own unique response, some might argue an overresponse, to my inner demons and circumstances. If I had not developed a humorous, clownish response to failures, from early elementary experiences with inferior grades, to failures in sports, embarrassment in music competitions, Boy Scouts (I could not get past Second Class scout because I could *not* memorize Morse Code), and other seemingly innocent arenas of competition, I would not have become the funny storyteller that I became. Whether my brother and sister remember it this way, whether friends or neighbors remember, is not too important. I remember it this way. And what was going on inside of me was far, far more troublesome, painful, and traumatizing than anyone, including my parents or classmates, could possibly have known. It is who I am. It is my unique journey that I choose to share in my storytelling.

---

**Why Some Personal Stories Don't Work**

1. The story is not funny.

2. The story does not have a clear point.

3. The story is self-centered or self-laudatory. Stories fail when the hero wins and the story seems self-indulgent. When the speaker wins all the time, the story simply isn't funny. But the story also needs a victory. In "Pine Tar," I include my later years as a successful college basketball player.

4. The story is too long. Audiences have a built-in inner clock.

5. The story is too maudlin or sappy. Emotion and pathos are critical ingredients, but too much touchy-feely, "poor me" sentiment is a killer.

---

# 13 GET TO THE POINT ALREADY!

How do we make a clear point through a story? That's a crucial question. Telling a personal story can irritate an audience unless there is a clear reason to be telling the story. Just a few years ago, a corporate speaker would often apologize for telling a personal story. "Forgive me for telling a personal story but ..." Attitudes have shifted and today audiences are accustomed to hearing about the personal lives of celebrities, politicians, movie stars, and sports stars. Not only are they accustomed to self-disclosure, but they expect and appreciate insights into a speaker's personal life. Where you are "coming from" is an important part of the relational dynamic of a speech. A personal story is welcomed today in most circles. However, a well-told personal story must have a clear point. Understanding why you are telling this particular story at this point in time is crucial for audience receptivity.

I love to launch into one of my stories, anticipating audience participation with laughter. Hearts and minds are opened through humor. And it is at that point that a more important exchange occurs between speaker and listener. The point of the story.

On most occasions the context allows me to be funny for a while and not worry about making a point or teaching a lesson. Eventually I feel the need to bring the audience into the purpose for the stories. The point can be made subtly or with force, depending on the occasion, the context, and other relational dynamics. The context always determines my approach. Last week I spoke to professional speakers about the value of storytelling, and to a group of salespeople for Jayco, the maker of campers and RVs. Next week I'll speak to my hometown Chamber of Commerce dinner, dressed in cowboy boots, jeans, and western shirt. And later in the week I will give a pep talk to the hometown high school football team before the final Homecoming game of the twentieth century. What a variety of contexts and dynamics!

How do we use our carefully developed stories in a wide variety of contexts and make a clear point in each circumstance? We do so by accurately reading the context, the audience, the event, the time and place, and the speaker.

- If the group is made up of schoolteachers and it is opening day of school, I assume the atmosphere is filled with anticipation of a new school year, excitement, and some anxiety, mixed with high hopes and fears. They are on edge and it's a perfect context for good humor to release that tension, to drive home important lessons, and to share my personal views as a speaker. That's why I have been invited to speak: to give my view of the topic at hand.

- An after-dinner program is usually wide open for humor and story. Very little message is expected by the listeners. If the audience is made up of salespeople at an annual meeting, the context is a bit more serious and the speaker is expected to provide information or insights that might help them be better salespersons during the coming months. The point of the story is very important. I use the same stories but change the emphasis of the point to be made.

- The audience may be small business owners, fast-food employees, a Chamber of Commerce, or a group of doctors or nurses. The makeup of the group changes the context and therefore the point of the story. But you must make a point.

## HOW TO MAKE A POINT

Here's how I make a point by using a story for teachers and school staff. The audience are teachers and staff with a life-long interest in and commitment to educational issues of various kinds. For example, there is a long-running debate in educational circles about the perceived value of strict grading or tracking, especially in lower grades. Years ago it was accepted that grades were handed out for performance, like my early report cards. In recent years research has revealed that human beings, especially young, immature minds, absorb information in a variety of ways. Many educators believe that strict measuring or grading may be harmful. Thus the emergence of more flexible styles in teaching that place less emphasis on immediate results. Under the old rules, when a child said "Two and two is five" the child failed and was given an F. Under the newer system, when a child says "Two and two is five" the teacher might say, "Oh, that's interesting. We'll discuss your answer tomorrow." In a recent workshop conducted by Ph.D. Janelle Barlow, an authority on creativity, I watched as a roomful of attendees found a dozen possible answers for the solution to $2 + 2$. For example, $2 + 2 = 3 + 1$ and $2 + 2 = 22$. Modern educational theory encourages teachers to allow more creativity and be less prone to punish or fail the student who does not always perform within the standard lines.

Teachers can be (bitterly) divided over these theories. When I speak to educational groups, I tell a story I call "The Canary Reader." This story reframes the entire issue to show how the child might feel in a more rigid environment, like the ones many of us experienced as children. In this story our little hero stands at the chalkboard as his friends are placed into certain reading groups. I exaggerate the importance of reading groups by adding that the local preacher would announce your name at the Sunday morning service if you were placed in the Redbird group.

> "The Redbirds, A students, future doctors and lawyers, had brand new books and a five-minute playtime. Then there were the Bluebirds, that's your B students ... future teachers and coaches." [Big laugh from teachers and coaches. Somehow they seem to agree that B students do in fact become teachers and coaches.]

> "Then there were the Robins, C students." [The audience anticipates who I might place in this lower group.] "That would be future politicians and salespeople."

> "So I'm standing at the chalkboard looking silly and realize I'm the only kid not in a group. So I said, 'Ms. Bell, did you forget me? What group am I in?'"

> "James, hon, I didn't forget you. You are in a special group."

Special education is another buzzword filled with connotations, and in this context there are often giggles and knowing smiles among teachers, and occasionally some serious reframing of viewpoints. By this time I have captured them with the lightness of humor and there is zero audience resistance. Therein lies the power of story. Educators see grading and tracking from the child's viewpoint and, more importantly, they grasp the reason we are spending time on this story. The story now has meaning.

But we are not done yet.

> "Which group is that?" I ask in my practiced childhood voice.
>
> "You're in the Canary reading group."
>
> "Who else is in that group?"
>
> "Hon, it's you and Elmer Joe Tackett." [Elmer is a fictional character I have already introduced in the speech.]

There are, of course, several reasons for placing children in groups of equal ability. However, in my reframing of this long-accepted practice, I am attempting to point out the other side for a few overly sensitive children, like me, who may be affected permanently.

Later in the program I tell another story, the story of my 30-year reunion. In the middle of that story I say rather casually, "As I looked around the room that night at all my childhood friends, Redbirds and Bluebirds, who were approaching fifty and retirement, it occurred to me that it doesn't make much difference what reading group you are in way back in the second grade." Now the purpose for spending valuable time on a childhood story is even more clear.

Over the years I have told this story a hundred times to teachers and staff during in-service training days at high schools. Hundreds of teachers have provided feedback on that story. Many have stated that it affirmed their own views about strict measuring. Many more have said that they must "rethink their viewpoints" on strict measuring. That's all a speaker can ask for. You are there to encourage new thinking or a search and process in the journey.

A woman approached me after a speech and said, "I was brought up Catholic. Our reading groups were Archangels, Guardian Angels, and ... Fallen Angels."

Similar childhood memories were stirred in her mind.

The lines about my 30-year reunion and the Fallen Angels were added later after many tellings and demonstrate how stories build over a period of time. Audience feedback is a wonderful source of humor material. The story is true, is embellished for live entertainment, reframes an issue, and purposely attempts to persuade the audience to a particular viewpoint.

## TAILORING THE POINT OR LESSON FOR DIFFERENT AUDIENCES

On the average you will discover, develop, and deliver dozens of your own stories over time. At some point you will realize that perhaps five or six of those stories are true keepers, and you will want to tell those stories on every occasion to different audiences. A minister addressing the same congregation each week faces a different challenge in story development. However, most ministers address many, many different audiences each year, as guest in other churches, at special meetings, annual conventions, denominational conferences, high school assemblies, and Rotary clubs. Stories can be developed for audiences other than the home congregation.

Using your highly developed stories in front of different audiences and in different contexts requires deriving a different lesson or point from the same story. Allow me to use "The Canary Reader" to show how I use it to emphasize different points for different audiences.

1. *Insurance sales convention:* In this context I have already described my growing-up years in Arkansas

as the second son of a football coach and my attempts at baseball, football, and the usual means of finding parental approval. I describe my frustration with academic pursuits and then tell the "Canary Reader" story. Whereas the point of the story to teachers and staff was the grading versus outcome-based teaching issue, I now emphasize an entirely different slant. The little hero in the story was placed in an inferior group, made to feel rather second-rate or dumb, a failure. When he went back to his 30-year reunion, he realized it wasn't as important as it seemed at the time.

The point? The speaker standing before them telling this story is an adult who spent the rest of his life reading, writing, storytelling, and in serious pursuit of knowledge as an adult. The message is that every child is a unique, once-in-a-universe human being. He found his own unique way to succeed in the world ... and you can too! I encourage them to use their own unique style and life journey to find their success.

2. *Customer service:* When I tell the story to business owners of fast-food chains, I focus on yet another aspect of the story. Fast-food employers all agree that their number-one problem is hiring, training, and maintaining good staff—usually young people in their first jobs. When I speak to this group, I have hinted to them that perhaps they should hire the young person with a happy personality and a big smile, someone who enjoys interacting with people, and not necessarily the most successful young person from an academic perspective. "You're not hiring a Ph.D. candidate, you are looking for a dependable, perky, happy kid to

face your customers. The class clown may be just the youngster you want."

3. *American Society for Curriculum Development:* Although this is an educational group, let's look again at this type of audience. "The Canary Reader" is obviously more suited for an educational audience than say, a political rally—just as your stories might be ideal for corporate, political, religious, high-tech, agriculture, health care, or other audiences. Probably no audience I would ever face (except for parents of second graders, which we'll look at next) could have been more appropriate than educators who actually determine the teaching styles and curriculum of America's children.

On a recent occasion I told "The Canary Reader" to that very appreciative and savvy group. That day I really "poured it on," as my father used to say about the Sunday morning sermon. A speech is a dance between speaker and audience. When the audience is perfectly in tune with the issue at hand, the speaker feels the extra adrenaline and responds like Michael Jordon in the final moments of a championship game. I poured myself into the story that day in an attempt to squeeze every nuance of meaning out of the experience of the child. They laughed heartily and then, at the end of the story, began a long ovation in the middle of the speech, not because I am any more talented or skillful as a storyteller or speaker than others, but because of the context.

Consider the contextual dynamics in the room that day; the Canary Reader returns to Arkansas as a successful writer, speaker, storyteller, and avid lifetime reader in pursuit of knowledge, growth, and God.

Context: Right speaker, right time, right audience, perfect story. Even further relational juices flowed that day because my older brother David, who is mentioned often as the perfect older brother, was in attendance as a longtime member of ASCD and Superintendent of Schools in Sheridan, Arkansas.

4. *Elementary school parents:* "The Canary Reader" provides relief for frustrated, well-meaning parents of children who struggle in their academic pursuits. They hear this story about a seemingly normal kid being placed in a special group due to bad performance, and realize the kid grew up to be a sane and semisuccessful human being. The parents get the story at a deep level and many have told me later that they plan to give their children a little slack in regard to school performance, or at least regarding the strictness of grading.

## THE POINT IS DETERMINED BY THE CONTEXT

Almost every story you create can be slanted toward a meaningful point for your audience. Remember, your best stories will be funny and will carry a certain weight due to sheer entertainment value. The point you make is viewed as extra added value from the speaker and does not have to be as profound as the Gettysburg Address. Allow some of the points to be subtle, perhaps even a bit hidden or cloaked in mystery. This allows the audience member to participate in the exploration of what it was like to experience the personal event the speaker is sharing.

In the three stories we have studied, "Facing Fishook," "The Canary Reader," and "Pine Tar," we've uncovered a wide variety of possible issues to emphasize, depending on the makeup of the audience.

**"Facing Fishook"**

1. Rite-of-passage life shaper
2. Father–son relationship
3. Sibling competition
4. Facing fears and breaking through them
5. Feminine savior
6. Shame in defeat or of unmanly fear
7. Questioning masculine styles
8. Questions about accepted truth
9. Find the Victory out of seeming defeat

**"The Canary Reader"**

1. Self-esteem issues
2. Challenges accepted views
3. Questions assumptions about measuring up
4. Opens discussion about learning modes
5. Allows parents to see uniqueness of each child
6. Opens discussion about ideas of success

**"Pine Tar"**

1. Explores adolescent fears
2. Sibling competition
3. Father as both mentor and challenger
4. Peer competition
5. Supreme ordeal
6. Transformation
7. Final victory

Your own personal stories, as well as other people's stories, must make one or preferably many clear points. Humor provides entertainment for the audience and serves to soften their hearts and to allow new information, new ideas, and new viewpoints to enter and hopefully stay a while.

# 14 DISCOVERING AND DELIVERING OTHER PEOPLE'S STORIES

ndividual stories are all around us. A speaker can use a contemporary OPS (Other People's Story) quickly and easily without the time required for development of personal stories. OPSs happen on a daily basis and you simply have to awaken your awareness to them. They can be told in an informal manner, and are not required to be funny—just fun and hopefully inspirational. Recall Susan Lucci, the daytime television star who had been nominated for an Emmy Award in 19 consecutive years. Year after year she lost to another actress. In that incredible story that lasted over 18 years of losing, a hero emerged. Finally, on her nineteenth nomination, the spell was broken and she won the Emmy. It made headlines worldwide and a tremendous victory was won, a victory originating out of almost two decades of losing. What a great story, and so easy to tell. Just tell it like it happened. After a few days, that story is out of the news and you can quickly find another one.

Chris Antley comes to mind. His is a story right out of the headlines that can work well in a speech or a Sunday sermon. He was a successful professional jockey and was even named Rider of the Year in 1986. That in itself is a success story. But Chris didn't become a household name just by being successful. He had to undergo the trials and tribulations of every hero.

Somewhere along the way Chris became addicted to drugs and alcohol. He gained weight, a professional hazard for a jockey, and by the mid 1990s was out of the profession. His father never lost faith in him. (Have you noticed how many fathers appear in stories? The Oedipal issue is deeply embedded in the human psyche and always will be; from Zeus to Apollo, and in my case Dionysius, the second son, to Luke Skywalker and Darth Vader.) Chris lay on his father's couch for two years, and he gained weight and lost his riding edge. Dad loved him anyway. One day Chris simply got up off the couch and started running. He ran all day. He ran all the next day and for almost six months until he had lost the baggage. Wayne Lukus, owner of a horse named Charismatic, knew Chris was a talented rider and gave him a chance to return to racing.

Chris rode Charismatic in the Kentucky Derby and won the second leg of the Triple Crown. His comeback event was worldwide news. From the Supreme Ordeal and the sympathy that comes with being the underdog, Chris Antley and Charismatic became headline news.

But the story goes even further.

Chris Antley and Charismatic were favorites in the Belmont Stakes, the third leg of the Triple Crown. The comeback kid on the horse from nowhere was a great story.

Down the stretch they came with Charismatic nose to nose for the lead, when suddenly the horse began to run with uneven strides. Something was wrong with the horse. Chris felt the champion stumble beneath him with only a few yards to the finish line. He pulled back on the reins, stopped the horse, and dismounted. Exhausted, he fell to the turf, struggled to hold onto the excited horse, got up, and pulled the horse's leg upward to remove weight from the injured bone, saving the bone from snapping and preventing the horse's destruction.

A terrible defeat just when ultimate victory was in sight?

Perhaps, but the heroic effort of Chris Antley made even bigger news than the eventual winner of the race. In defeat, the horse was saved by the quick thinking of the comeback kid.

In the stories right out of the news of Susan Lucci and Chris Antley, we see how success flows out of defeat or failure. Just tell those stories in your own words. As one event fades out of the news, move on to newer OPSs.

Where's the humor? Interestingly enough I find that when telling the stories of other people, humor is not a critical requirement. Why? Well, the hero wins in OPSs and that is not funny. Humor happens when the hero fails.

Humor is essential when telling stories about our own adventures, for it takes the focus away from our victories and makes fun of our defeats. The humor changes them back to victory, if only an artistic or psychological victory.

Quite often, while watching the evening news or a documentary of some kind, I'll see a story that brings a tear to my eye. A young man with a noticeable birthmark on his face plays outfield for the LA Dodgers; a former beauty queen from Oregon looses all her hair through some rare disease and turns her tragedy into victory by creating self-image programs for high school girls. Stories are literally all around us every day, and all you have to do is develop a mythic sense, a sense of drama and story in people's lives.

That's why there is no excuse for a speaker to tell an old, worn-out story that everyone has heard. It happens all the time. I once watched and listened in horror as a big-name author, but admittedly a new speaker, spoke to 2,000 of

America's top professional speakers—a tough crowd—and told three very old, worn-out stories. He might have gotten away with one. But telling two, and then three, was unmitigated disaster. What were the stories? Well, you remember the one about the guy walking on the beach, throwing starfish into the sea? Right. That poor starfish has been trying to crawl out of the sea for years.

I think the other one might have been the old saw about a large pile of horse manure and the little optimistic boy digging around the pile who said, "With all this manure, there must be a pony in here somewhere."

Many years ago I heard two consecutive speakers tell that particular story to the same audience. The second speaker was aware that the first speaker had used the story, but told the story anyway. The audience felt insulted.

As a beginning speaker, I admit that I often used old stories. But over a period of time I eliminated threadbare stories and made it a point to use only personal stories or stories of daily heroes that I found and developed myself. It's not only more effective, but it's easier to tailor a story to your particular audience when it's one they haven't heard before.

## LITERATURE, HEROES, AND CHICKEN SOUP

In my first job as a writer, I worked for veteran speaker and television personality Art Linkletter. He had a daily radio show called *The Art of Positive Thinking*. It was my job to discover, develop, and write 32 stories per month into script form. I now realize that those hours in the library were very well spent. Digging through magazines, books, and just about any information source I could get my hands on, I set my eye and ear for daily heroes like Susan Lucci and Chris Antley.

Working for Art Linkletter was fun. Not only was he one of the great legends of television but he was a true professional when it came to humor with story. During that time I became aware that every day of our lives we see heroic stories all around us. Mark Victor Hansen and Jack Canfield thought it would be a good idea to gather 101 of these everyday hero stories and publish them in a book they would call *Chicken Soup for the Soul.* That collection of stories became wildly popular and eventually landed on *The New York Times* best-seller list at number one. Each story in the book is inspirational and follows the hero's journey model, with a call, a challenge, and a victorious solution.

This concept has become part of our cultural vocabulary, and we now hear references to a "Chicken Soup" type of story. At this writing, more than a dozen *Chicken Soup* books have been published. All are successful and many more are scheduled for publication. Most of the stories used in this series feature the key element of successful storytelling—the Hero's Journey.

*Chicken Soup*-type stories are excellent for a speaker to use on the platform. While they may not be considered serious literature with their formulaic and (some say) unrealistically happy endings, the public responds to these stories, much as they did to Horatio Alger stories in another generation. Critics of *Chicken Soup*-style stories fail to look beyond the familiar three phases. These stories do follow the cyclical pattern of Hero's Quest stories, but that doesn't mean they are not realistic. We need go no further than the great Joyce in defense of the three phases. Joyce, the foremost literary genius of the English language, understood the proper use of the three phases. *Ulysses* and *Finnegan's Wake* are based on the cyclical movement of the Hero's Journey. His classic but difficult to understand *Ulysses* is based on *The Odyssey* of Homer, perhaps the heart and soul of Hero's Quest mythology. The three phases are deeply embedded within the story. And *Finnegan's Wake* is based on the same cyclical hero phases.

Joyce, who was entrenched in these three phases, was anything but formulaic. Joyce understood every kind of story. *Dubliners,* his series of vignettes about life in Ireland, contains slice of life stories that have no clear-cut meaning, no Supreme Ordeal, and no happy ending or wrap-up. Joyce understood both types of story and used both effectively in his art.

## WHERE DO WE FIND EVERYDAY HEROES?

Daniel J. Boorstein in his book *The Seekers* writes about the Homeric epics and states, "The modern reader may feel disappointed that the *Odyssey* does not hold him in suspense but always has a familiar outcome—suggesting the aim is not to surprise but to remind."

Hero stories remind us of what we already suspect is true about life's continuous journey.

Stories of a more literary bent, such as the works of Joyce Carol Oates, Raymond Chandler, John Updike, and other literary giants, are wonderful reading. But for stories that will work well in oral delivery, look for tales that lend themselves to a clear point or lesson. Here's how I discovered a story that was so perfect for inspirational storytelling that I used it for years. It never failed to move people in the audience.

Some years ago I was watching the evening news with my son, Ryan. At the end of the sports news we saw one of those brief can-you-believe-it pieces that caught our attention. We watched as an out-of-focus film of a high school football game highlighted a particular boy making three tackles in a row, the last one a sack of the quarterback. Then the film cut to a basketball game highlighting the same boy playing center ... and that's when we noticed something very, very unusual. The boy had only one leg.

His name was Carl Joseph, and I learned more of his story later from Hall of Fame football player Dan Dierdorf. Carl was born with only one leg. But he decided not to let that reality affect his life. He was the defensive nose tackle on the high school football team in Madison, Florida, and a center on the basketball team. He had learned to hop up and down the floor and was a good player. He was the shot putter on the track team, and one day at a track meet he asked the coach if he could try the high jump. The coach, slightly shocked, said "Carl, I've seen you do some incredible things, but I don't think a one-legged person can high jump."

"I've been practicing, Coach. Let me try."

Carl entered the high jump that day and jumped 6 feet 2 inches ... and won the event. (A side note here: In my telling of the story, I don't reveal to the audience that Carl had only one leg until after they knew that he was center on the basketball team, nose tackle on the football team, and shot putter on the track team. Just before I tell about his high-jumping prowess, I say casually, "Oh, did I mention that Carl Joseph was born with only one leg?" Then I pause and let it sink in.)

Consider that story. Carl is a real human being. His slice-of-life story may not be literature—it's tasty *Chicken Soup*—but it's true. The story is a natural winner, and that's the kind you must find and learn to tell. For several years I told the story using the three phases and it never failed to have the desired effect on the audience: awe, appreciation, admiration, and inspiration to overcome all obstacles and conquer one's own challenges. Some might call it sappy or touchy-feely. But if you talked to Carl he would say it was real life, his life. His accomplishments are the result of very hard work. It was not touchy-feely at all for him.

Formulaic, a contrived ending? Not if you lived it and through hard work and sheer courage made your story end happily.

Carl received a football scholarship to Bethune-Cookman College. He dealt with an uncommon challenge without a whimper. He is a living, breathing hero and the way we developed the story, the audience felt a three-phase process of call, Supreme Ordeal, and victory every time he stepped on the court or the football field.

After seeing Carl's story on television, I wanted to know more about him. I made a few phone calls to his football coach in Madison, Florida and filled out the details.

I introduce a light touch of humor right after the stunning realization of his real-life situation in the line, "Coach, let me enter the high jump."

"Carl, I've seen you do some incredible things" [showing praise and approval of the hero] "but there is no way a one-legged person can high jump." The coach's remark revealed an intimacy with the hero; the line is fully accepted as good-natured by the coach and not as a put-down.

If you are going to tell stories about other people, events, and places, it remains essential that the stories contain within them the Hero's Journey model and just a taste of *Chicken Soup.*


## THE HEART OF A LION

Here's another OPS that I mentioned briefly in an earlier chapter. Midori Ito of Japan was favored to win a gold medal in figure skating in the 1992 Olympics. She was the first woman skater to consistently land the very difficult triple axle jump in competition, and the entire nation of Japan pinned their hopes for a first gold medal on her tiny frame. The night finally arrived and she skated onto the ice before worldwide television.

Ito's program went smoothly as she grew closer to the much anticipated triple turn in midair. Gaining speed, she flew down the center of the arena, dipped, and sprang high into the air, twirled three times, landed—and fell to the ice. The hero Accepts the Journey, Faces the Challenge, and in the Supreme Ordeal fails by falling in a heap on the ice. There was a gasp in the arena and around the world. Defeat.

Or was it? Midori Ito pulled herself together and, knowing her chances for a gold medal were left on the ice, regained her composure and moved back into the program. Toward the end, one of the announcers commented, "Little Midori Ito is really moving down the ice, you don't think she would try another …?"

Before he could complete the sentence, the little girl with the heart of a lion suddenly sprang high in the air, twirled three times, and landed perfectly. That incredible feat moved her back up to third place for a bronze medal. She became a national treasure in Japan. From the agony of defeat and failure, she showed uncommon courage and found the victory.

I have told that story on several occasions. It has a mesmerizing effect on the audience, whether they have never heard of Midori Ito or they remember the event itself. It is such a classic story of the hero with heart that it works with every conceivable audience. There is more. During opening ceremonies for the 1996 Olympics in Nagano, Japan, I watched along with millions around the world as all of the teams marched in the always-emotional parade. The Olympic torch arrived in the stadium, but the final keeper of the flame, the one honored to light the giant flame, had remained a secret. On the platform that night in Japan stood a tiny little figure skater with the heart of a lion, a true hero—Midori Ito.

Humans are inspired when we see everyday people do extraordinary things. When real life shows us courage—victory snatched from the jaws of defeat—we dare not brush it off as contrived or a merely unrealistic happy ending. We call it heroic.

As a speaker, you can assume that the power of persuasion can be used to inspire others to be better, to overcome, to try again and to find the victories in life's challenges. Those are the qualities to seek in the delivery of other people's stories.

---

### Five Steps for Developing Stories

1. Develop your Daily Hero Sense by noticing stories that appear in the news every day. Cut them out of the paper or jot down some notes and put them in a folder or computer file. I have a folder full of great stories and can use them at any moment. OPSs do not have to be funny.

2. Notice the three phases of the journey. Write them down. Reflect upon the event and become clear on what about the story caught your attention. Then you can say, "Here are three things I learned from this great hero."

3. Tell the story to friends and family. "Did you see that incredible story ...." is a good way to start. Recall it a few times and measure the response. Find lightness and appropriate humor.

---

4. Make a phone call or two to research the story. You will then have information that brings the story to life, details such as "Coach, let me enter the high jump ... ."

5. Use each story in the right context for the right audience.

# 15 BEYOND SKILL AND TOWARD SOUL IN DELIVERY

---

The Broadmoor Hotel in Colorado Springs has been a regular stop on the speaking circuit for many years. I drop by there every year or so for an association or corporate meeting. The Broadmoor may have witnessed more corporate business presentations over the years than any other hotel or resort in America. To bring a new twist to an old cliché, "If these walls could talk ... they would have nothing to say." Corporate speaking is traditionally the most painfully boring venue in the use of the English language this side of C-Span.

My last trip was a memorable one due to a most incredible display of boring corporate speaking. I was scheduled for an 11 a.m. wrap-up speech to about 400 conference attendees for an association in the financial community that will remain nameless. The program listed six speakers, an unusually high number of general session speakers, one after another in the same auditorium. The first speaker was introduced in a very formal fashion. He walked to the rostrum with manila folder in hand and quietly placed it on the stand. He then opened it and pulled out an overhead transparency and placed it on the overhead projector, which immediately flashed scripted words upon the big screen behind him. The speech that followed consisted of the words on the screen behind him delivered verbatim, pausing only to change the transparency when necessary. After about 30 minutes he closed the manila folder, uttered a terse "Thank you," and walked off the stage.

The next speaker was introduced and proceeded in the very same manner, as did the next four speakers. The audience strolled in and out of the room, read the paper, chatted in the back of the room where coffee and water were served, or walked outside for a smoke break.

These speakers were intelligent, professional men with important things to say. The scripts were well-written and the words on the screen contained important information pertaining to the future of interest rates, potential earnings, possible mergers, trends, and more. Although the men were articulate, some even skillful as speakers, and had pertinent information, as a speaker, I could not help but notice the lack of audience attention. The audience may have been interested in the speakers, but the speaking style generally used in corporate America is totally inadequate for authentic engagement of an audience. The lacking ingredients in the six corporate speeches—the accepted style of corporate speaking—are human emotion, passion for the message, enthusiasm, and most important, soul. There was no humor, story, vernacular language, or slang—just a solid formal barrier between speaker and audience.

I was introduced, the only outside or professional speaker, and faced a very tired audience. Using a style of speaking that I call Relationship Speaking and that Walt Whitman referred to as participatory style, I approached the audience.

In Relationship Speaking, the primary purpose is to break down the natural barrier between speaker and audience. The speaker does this through certain techniques that are more instinctual than skillful, more mystery than mastery, more charismatic than cosmetic.

From the very first, my body language signaled something different. I walked casually to the stage, smiling at the audience, but rather than climbing up on the stage, I had arranged for a wireless, handheld mike. I strode onto the floor of the auditorium and said, "Did I ever tell ya'll about the time my father decided it was time for me to play football ...?" Every person in the room perked up. There was an instant flow of energy into the room, attendees smiled, and a few people looked up from conversations in the back of the room. What? What did he say? Who is this? In contrast to the corporate style, I was a shock to the system. I was off and running with stories, humor, and anecdotes delivered in an informal style that invited audience participation through laughter, emotional connection, and therefore, engagement. A critic could say, "Sure, they understood you were the fluff speaker, that the important stuff was over and it's entertainment time." It depends on what we mean by "fluff." I happen to think that numbers, charts, graphs, percentages, and so on are rather fluffy, because they are all going to change within a month or so and certainly by next year's meeting. The stories I was about to introduce are symbolic and filled with mythical and therefore eternal truths for those who choose to hear and absorb. But that is not the point really. We're talking about speaking styles, one stiff, rigid, formal, and controlled, the other loose, bending, informal, and relaxed.

## TEAPOT VERSUS RELATIONSHIP SPEAKING

There are basically two styles of speaking, with countless combinations of both. Alan Watts said, "Every reality can be expressed in two diametrically opposite ways." That is true of the art of oratory.

The first style is a mechanical style that places emphasis on words, information, charts, and graphs and is designed to disseminate information. The second is a more informal style that places emphasis on story, symbol, humor, and passion for a message. Both styles can be found in the corporate world, in politics, education, speaking, and preaching.

Both styles of speaking are proper, depending upon the context, and both can be used, depending upon the intention of the speaker in engaging the audience. The professional speaker's purpose is different from that of a corporate leader, a professor, or a political speaker. Generally, the professional speaker's intention is to make the deepest emotional connection with the audience, a connection that invites the participation, emotionally and physically, of the listener. Laughter is audience participation, and that is why humor is perhaps the very best means of winning over and engaging an audience.

From schoolteacher to corporate leader to political candidate, the intention of the speaker and the context determine the choice of speaking style.

Corporate speakers feel compelled to maintain a certain amount of decorum, and it is unlikely that a CEO will cross over the imaginary line from blue-suited dignity that purposely maintains the speaker–audience barrier. Unfortunately, the audience will remain basically disinterested, disconnected, and unmoved.

However, we have seen numerous examples to the contrary in corporate leaders such as Lee Iacocca, who saved the Chrysler Corporation; in the military, with General Schwartzkopf; and in politics, with Bill Clinton and Ronald Reagan, the originator of the aw-shucks demeanor. But the vast majority in these realms choose a formal, rigid, scripted, and reasoned style of public speaking. They dismiss the use of humor and are loath to self-disclose for fear their vulnerability may be misinterpreted as weakness.

Each of the highly successful leaders mentioned (of course, there are many, many more) uses humor and self-disclosure and just the proper amount of vulnerability. If a corporate leader, manager, professor, minister, or teacher is willing to break through the barrier that exists between speaker and audience, he or she must move toward, if not totally embrace, a more relational style of speaking.

## RELAXED, FOLKSY, AND FRIENDLY

The uniquely American style of oratory—informal, folksy, friendly, with free use of vernacular and humor—evolved out of the American theater and was further refined in Protestant pulpits. This style emerged out of an atmosphere that Whitman touted in the new world of democracy. Egalitarian values were sweeping America in the pre–Civil War era. This new oratorical style, befitting the age of every man and woman created equal (in spite of the mounting tensions of slavery), was becoming popular in New York pulpits. A particular preacher named Henry Ward Beecher drew thousands of people on Sunday mornings. Beecher was a celebrity in an age before mass media or television.

Beecher's style was in stark contrast to the previous styles of acting and oratory that made their way over from the European stage, where actors were entrenched in ancient theatrical traditions. The European actor stood on stage, in just the right place, and with one hand on hip, with carefully modulated voice, recited Hamlet while twirling the other hand in the air, like a teapot. Thus, the Teapot style of oratory.

David S. Reynolds explores both styles in his book, *Walt Whitman's America*. He describes the style of Beecher and its effect on the audience. "A dark-haired, broad browed clergyman walks out onto a pulpit platform that reaches well forward into the congregation. With a look of winning benignity, he surveys the nearly three thousand people who have traveled to Brooklyn's Plymouth Church to hear him. He has no script, no notes. He begins his sermon with a joke and a story. His listeners are enthralled. They laugh and cry their way through the sermon."

Let's examine Reynolds' descriptive statement about Beecher.

"Enthralled" is another word for entranced, or trance; the state of being we called a trance, discussed earlier that is brought about by story. Reynolds' description of the listeners' reaction, "they laughed and cried," describes a totally engaged audience riding high on emotions.

Beecher was a pioneer in the emerging style. Keep in mind the contrasting styles in speaking that day at the Broadmoor as we examine Beecher's style in five areas:

1. *Body placement.* Beecher built and designed the Brooklyn Church and purposely had the pulpit built far out into the congregation to be near the people. His physical presence near the people is similar to my walking into the audience that day at the Broadmoor. Most experienced speakers know the value of body placement in the room. Break down the physical barrier between audience and speaker. Become one with the audience by moving physically into the seating area. Whereas in the past preachers were solidly ensconced behind a pulpit, the modern preacher uses a lapel mike and moves in and through the audience.

2. *"With a look of winning benignity,"* Beecher used subtle body language to communicate a oneness with the crowd, "I am one of you." The very posture and car-

riage of the speaker send multilevel messages. Will Rogers may be the best example of the "good ole boy" approach. Ronald Reagan perfected the "aw-shucks" style with his natural charm and humility. Bill Clinton used this technique when he approached the ropes and made physical contact with people through handshaking. Corporate leaders may feel the need to intimidate their audiences and perhaps, on certain occasions, it is the preferred demeanor. However, a presenter will be accepted more readily when using body language that invites warmth and a friendly response.

3. *"He has no script, no notes."* Sermons during this era were traditionally long and boring. Their purpose was to teach church doctrines and admonish the congregation. Beecher's purpose was not to teach with words or reasoned ideas about doctrines. His purpose was to touch the hearts and engage the emotions of the audience with passion for his message, delivered through stories that added emotion to his delivery. Without notes, he made continuous eye contact. This revolutionary style was even more important in a time when High Church preachers read sermons from scripts prepared through hours of arduous sermon preparation taught by seminaries. Beecher used stories and anecdotes to add spontaneous humor.

Notes can be used effectively as long as the speaker breaks away from them and engages the audience. Gazing at notes disengages the audience momentarily. No stand-up comic I know of uses notes, nor does a top actor. Preachers often refer to notes and Bible references. Corporate speakers often read scripts verbatim. Politicians use the dreaded teleprompter, set up just in front of their eyes, creating a glassy-eyed stare toward the actual audience.

4. *"He begins his sermon with a joke and a story."* Beecher used many personal stories, sharing personal failures with his audiences, revealing private fears and doubts, even questioning either the power of God or his own personal faith, an unprecedented method in his day. Humor is a magical potion for large crowds. Laughter is a group dance that builds community, love, acceptance, and joyful feelings that emanate through an audience.

5. *"They laugh and cry their way through the sermon."* These are very revealing words. They laugh "through" the sermon implies a continuous line of humor. Henry Ward Beecher was partly storyteller and comedian. He was willing to challenge the status quo, break down accepted barriers, and engage the audience to the point of riotous laughter and hot tears. Beecher's breakthrough style was in contrast to the formal, rigid, stiff-collared approach of other sermonizers of his day. The choice was between reasoned ideas and emotion, between strict doctrinal theory and symbols through story, or perhaps between the law of God and the love and forgiveness of God. Beecher chose the latter and created a sensation in a time of rigid adherence to dogma.

As a child, I was exposed to many, many hours of southern Baptist preaching handed down from generation to generation virtually unchanged from the breakthrough styles of Henry Ward Beecher, Elias Hicks, and the famed Boston Methodist preacher Edward Taylor Thompson. Emerson and Whitman, as well as Thoreau, flocked to hear

Thompson, whom Emerson described as "the Shakespeare of the American pulpit."

I absorbed thousands of hours of passionate, enthusiastic, story-centered preaching that demanded a response either inwardly or outwardly from the audience. This participation of the audience was brought about by the chosen style of the orator. It seems obvious enough that my personal style of speaking emerged from those childhood hours of listening to southern preaching, full of friendly body language, stories, humor, self-disclosure, and compassion.

The Teapot style is formal and mechanical, focused on words, ideas, arguments, agendas, and ideologies. It is rational and reasoned and takes itself very seriously. The speaker is offering information and connects with the brain of the audience.

The Relationship style is fun, spontaneous, informal, story-centered, humor-filled, and in fact does not take itself too seriously. The speaker takes the audience beyond reasoned thinking, beyond ideas, and connects with the heart and soul.

The primary focus of the Relationship style is to break down the barrier between speaker and audience and then to persuade the audience toward the speaker's viewpoint.

| Characteristics of Teapot Style | Characteristics of Relational Speaking |
|---|---|
| Performance | Presence |
| Formal | Informal |
| Scripted | Free-wording |
| Rigid | Pliable |
| Rational | Transrational |
| Serious | Playful |
| Narrow | Open |

| Characteristics of Teapot Style | Characteristics of Relational Speaking |
|---|---|
| Superior | Egalitarian |
| Cold | Warm |
| Dry | Wet |
| Separate Components | Whole |
| Information | Emotion |
| Numbers | Symbols |
| Graphs | Poetry |

## FINDING THE PROPER BALANCE

I purposely exaggerated the Teapot style by choosing as an example an extreme case of corporate formality, rigidity, word-only focus, and lack of passion. The impact on the audience was predictable. There is nothing for the audience to engage with or participate in. Corporate speakers, preachers, trainers, or schoolteachers will connect with their listeners in direct proportion to their willingness and ability to move toward Relationship psychology.

In all fairness, we must admit that an orator can lean too far toward Relationship speaking. A speaker may become too bound up in emotion, story, humor, or enthusiasm, and have no rational, reasonable, or clear point.

While researching oratorical styles, on several occasions I tuned in contemporary preachers during their Sunday morning TV programs. The Beecher style is alive and well and is, at times, carried to an extreme. The Reverend Jesse Duplantis of New Orleans is a good example. Rev. Duplantis is a popular preacher who uses enthusiasm, story, self-revelation, and humor—perhaps too much humor. He is a natural comedian who entertains the congregation with nothing-to-hide, self-deprecatory stories. In that context, much of his humor seems inappropriate. Whereas my favorite standup comic, Sinbad's funny line, "Mama hit me so hard ... my butt fell off!" is an easily acceptable line in a comedy context, Rev. Duplantis' references to diarrhea, bad breath, flatulence, and loss of sexual prowess, although all done with humor, seem extreme.

A different form of exaggeration is employed by the "charismatic" preachers of the South, who demand participation by the audience. An African-American woman at the Holy Ghost Revival in Memphis demonstrated rare genius in the domain of enthusiasm, verbal power, body language, passion, and admonition, stirring the congregation to a responsive frenzy. Unfortunately, there was little reason, understanding, or organization of ideas in her presentation.

One of the best examples of reason, ideas, rational organization, and fiery enthusiasm fueled by passion for the message, combined with top-quality humor through story, is Dr. Anthony Campolo of St. Davids, Pennsylvania. Campolo has served as a private counselor for President Clinton, and openly shed tears at the famous White House prayer breakfast at which Clinton made his most heartfelt apology for the Monica Lewinsky affair. Campolo is a rare speaker, achieving the proper balance between the Teapot style and Relationship speaking, between reason and enthusiasm, information and symbol.

---

### Creating Balance

Depending on the context (a banquet, corporate meeting, annual convention, or Sunday morning service), the speaker must strive toward a proper mix of styles. Proper balance between both speaking styles is the ideal.

---

Using an imagined scale of 1 to 10 (with 1 representing the relational characteristics and 10 representing a rigid Teapot style), rate your own style of speaking.

1---------------------X----------------------------10.

A corporate context calls for dissemination of information. But a 10 on the scale is extremely rigid. You may want to adjust your style and tone and move toward a more balanced 5 or 6. A minister who remains in an extreme style of emotion, passion, and enthusiasm (1) may wish to seek balance by moving toward more reasoned ideas.

Finding the right balance and placing it in the right context is critical to your success in speaking.

Body placement (Separated or Connected)
1--------------------------------------------------10.

Body language (Formal or Informal)
1--------------------------------------------------10.

Content (Information or Story and Symbol)
1--------------------------------------------------10.

Style (Emotion or Reasoned Ideas)
1--------------------------------------------------10.

The corporate speakers at the Broadmoor that day had specific information to pass along. The traditional style of speaking they used is formal and word- and number-oriented.

It would be improper for one of those speakers to suddenly shift dramatically in style and tell funny stories, ad lib, or walk into the audience to share his or her heartfelt ideas. However, a speaker who shifts toward a more participatory style will have dramatic impact on the audience. Opening with a brief personal story will gain the attention of the audience and allow them to see the speaker as a fellow human being. Moving off of the script for a moment; taking the microphone in hand and walking away from the podium and relating to the audience; adding a bit of spontaneous humor about those standing in the back of the room talking; all will go a long way in changing the dynamics in the room.

Finally, be willing to tell a story. You'll be glad you did.

# 16 BASIC TIPS FOR POWERFUL SPEAKING

Not long ago I spoke to 1,300 K through 12 teachers in Denver during their annual in-service training day. Through my personal stories I challenged them to Find the Victory every day during the school year. With stories like "Facing Fishhook," "The Canary Reader," and others, I showed them how all of our journeys are heroic. Find the Victory was my message and story power was the means through which I delivered this message.

As we saw in Chapter 15, the style in which we choose to deliver a speech is extremely important. Our material or content is very important. It has been said often that it doesn't matter what you say, it's all in how you say it. That's too cynical for me. I believe that what you say is of crucial importance, that both what you say and how you say it are of equal value.

Someone has noted accurately that golf is a game with two completely different parts; the golf swing is one very complicated mechanical move, and the act of putting the ball a few feet or even a few inches is quite another athletic act. Both are essential in the game. But when you think about it, the golf swing that can send a ball hundreds of yards in the proper direction is totally unrelated to the far more simple act of putting the ball on the grass two or three feet. (Okay, I admit it, putting may be the hard part of golf.)

Speaking is that way too. The message is one thing, and it is crucial to high-impact speaking. But how it is delivered is a totally different thing. We have focused this study on the *how* and not the *what* in speaking. We have seen that story, with its potential for symbolism and use of innate universal archetypes, is a powerful way to deliver your message, whatever that message may be. Our primary focus is *how* you deliver your message, not *what* your message might be. That's up to you.

Here are some basic tips that will make you a more effective speaker.

You may not aspire to the highest level of professional speaking. Perhaps you are a teacher, salesperson, school board member, minister, or lawyer. In your chosen profession you use words, language, stories, and symbols to persuade your audience to your point of view. If you are an experienced pro, it is likely you are aware of these tips. But for a beginning speaker, these tips are valuable.

## USE A MICROPHONE WHENEVER POSSIBLE

Always use a movable microphone. Body language is a powerful communication tool. Don't stand behind a podium in one spot like a talking dummy when you can move around on the platform. In order to move around you'll need either a handheld microphone or a lavaliere, meaning attached to the lapel.

Think about it; what is your chief tool in the communication task? Sound. I once attended a meeting of professional speakers at which the newly inducted president approached the podium with an attached microphone, proceeded to push it downward and out of the way, and said," I just hate those things!" I knew immediately that our new president was not an experienced speaker. He was a talented actor and veteran of television commercials, but it was obvious he lacked experience in facing an audience, commanding their attention, and sustaining it with one tool: the sound of his voice.

Learn to use a microphone like a professional. Hold it just below your chin so the audience can see your full face and mouth. Hold it close and be certain that the volume is very high, or "hot." You want the full volume of your voice to fill that room, even when you are whispering (or perhaps most importantly when you are using soft tones).

I use the microphone as a prop. It becomes a baseball bat in the Fishhook story, a baton in the football story, a golf club, a stick of dynamite, or a spontaneous tool for whatever need I have.

The microphone, your medium of sound, is your most important tool.

## LIGHTS, PLEASE!

At a recent speaking engagement, I was standing on a huge auditorium stage. The lights above were inconsistent, so before the meeting began I walked the stage and located the light spots, literally. At crucial points in my speech I made certain that I stood squarely in one of the well-lit areas. Why? We saw earlier that facial expressions play a crucial role in humor. I can twist my lips, wiggle my nose, frown, look surprised, stunned, innocent, frightened, or sad, all with facial expressions. The audience must see these subtleties clearly. In an auditorium, I must find the best lighting, stand in it, and deliver the line, "That ball is coming right at your head." Pause. Eyes widen, head turns slightly, mouth agape. Titters of laughter at the expression on my face. Next line: "Right at my head?" Different tone of voice, and we're back to the use of the sound system; different facial expression, subtle but clear under the lights. This scene creates more laughter as it builds. Sound and lighting play crucial parts in the success of this scene.

## WHAT ABOUT THE USE OF NOTES?

One of the most effective speakers I've ever seen and heard uses notes. Her name is Rosita Perez, CPAE Speakers Hall of Fame, Cavett Award Winner, and simply a stunning presence on the platform. She puts a table on the stage and places notes down on the table that she refers to occasionally. She is a spellbinder and simply one of the best speakers I've seen. It just goes to show you that for every rule, there is someone who can break it in spectacular fashion.

For most speakers, it is probably best if you can avoid the use of notes. There is a temptation to rely too much on the notes and break eye contact with the audience every time you look down. Furthermore, that mesmerizing and trance-forming quality in speaking we are looking for, is lessened when we look down, pause, and continue. I suggest you don't use notes unless you have a special gift like Rosita Perez. Speaking is a mystery. As an example of how strange and unique every occasion is, I once saw Rosita close a program by dropping her note card, losing her place, then tripping over the microphone cord, and as a result receiving a powerful standing ovation. Do not try this at home. She is a professional.

## HOW TO OPEN THE SPEECH

"Thank you for that wonderful introduction. It is so good to be here today in Iowa. I just love Iowa ... My wife's third cousin used to live somewhere in Iowa, and I love corn, so I feel right at home."

This speaker is desperately trying to find common ground with the audience. It's proper to establish a "shared common experience," to use Erickson's phrase. It is not always easy to do. It is the right thing to do.

How do we do it?

Let's look at an example of being observant, taking a risk, and going for a super opening line for a unique event. At the teacher's training event mentioned at the start of this chapter, Deb Haviland, the meeting planner, was seated beside me in the front row as we watched the audience pour in. The front rows were last to fill and I noticed what appeared to be four football coaches (coaching shorts, white socks, T-shirts) in the fourth row. Football coaches usually dive for the back row. Next, if you really want to know, sit the veteran high school teachers; veteran elementary teachers are next; then as we move forward, high school humanities, then hard sciences, and finally, by default, in the front rows, usually sit first-year elementary teachers.

I was introduced, walked with my cordless mike to the front of the stage, looked directly at the coaches, and said, "If you boys could have torn yourselves away from the doughnut table a few minutes earlier, you wouldn't have to sit in the front."

They exploded with laughter, for I learned later that they had said the very same thing to each other and that had, in fact, been the reason they were in the front. The audience howled, knowing full well that the coaches usually sit in the back.

It was a bit of a risk on my part, but it worked beautifully. I won the coaches over (they can be resistant to a message like mine, urging teachers, coaches, and staff to rethink measuring, grading, and therefore fierce competition) and used them several times as "call-back" humor points.

I received a rousing standing ovation that day, even though I said some very challenging things to teachers, coaches, administration, and staff.

The importance of your opening line cannot be underestimated. The professional speaker is there to hit a home run, not just a single or a double. Take a calculated risk, be prepared (I made sure through Ms. Haviland that the four guys were actually coaches), and hit that home run early.

## The "Good Morning!" Curse

Probably the worst way to begin a speech is to walk out after the introduction and say "Good morning!" All agree the first few seconds of your appearance to the audience are extremely important. The audience will size you up, watch your body language as you approach the microphone, make a judgment about your clothes and hair, and some will decide immediately whether they like you or not. That may seem unfair to the speaker, but it's the way people think. You can use that quick audience assessment to your benefit. If you use proper body language and know exactly what to say in those first crucial seconds, you can win over the entire audience just as easily as you could lose them.

You have done your homework. You are fully aware of the audience makeup, size, gender breakdown, general educational level, the history of the event, their expectations, the time and place, their awareness of who you are as the speaker and a bit of your intention from the introduction.

I was not kidding when I said probably the worst opener in the world is the often used, "Good morning." It seems to fall flat on every occasion. The audience is a bit stunned at such a personal greeting and a few extroverts utter a desultory "Ga, 'mornin?" The speaker, who correctly is attempting to assume his or her role as leader of the session, feels obligated to create more enthusiasm and scolds the audience by saying, "Oh, come on! You can do better than that! GOOD MORNING!"

The audience, now feeling like an angry parent has disciplined them, is forced to scream, "Good morning!" We've all seen this numerous times and it seems to create instant bad vibes.

It's even worse if the CEO or boss is the speaker, and still worse if the speaker is an outsider and the CEO is sitting in the front row with the entire management team. The employees witness an outside speaker scolding the CEO. Bad karma.

## Possible Openers

Remembering the critical context factor, your intuitive reading of the many relational dynamics of a particular event, let's look at some winning ways to open a speech.

*Tell a Story:* My favorite way to open a speech, and I hope it is obvious by now, is to tell a story. Story instantly brings the audience into your frame of reference, and you can hold them as long as it is constructed in the proper way. A personal story will contain just enough self-revelation that your audience will begin to feel comfortable with you, understand a bit of your past history, and sense where you are coming from. For example, "My father was a football coach in Arkansas ..." is a brief statement, but the audience is given concrete information about my past and their imagination is activated. First they learn that I am from Arkansas, a southerner, raised in a sports environment, in the home of a coach. Quite often a ripple of laughter will run through the audience as they imagine what it might be like to be the son of the local football coach. At that point I can add the next line, "…and if you know anything about the South you know that football was more important than the First Baptist Church."

My southern or hillbilly twang is revealed to the audience and my body language has already sent a message that this will be a relaxed and informal speech. Within two lines, much has been revealed about the speaker and several laugh lines have been built in within seconds of the opening line.

The phrase, "Did I ever tell you about the time …" is an interesting way to begin a speech. The listener may never have met the speaker, but people recognize the playfulness involved in that phrase. It sends a message of informality and also lets the audience know that the speaker feels in control, confident, and comfortable.

*Use a Daily Hero Story:* For speakers who face the same audience, for example, a preacher, schoolteacher or college professor, different stories can be developed. This is a good time for one of the Other People's Stories that you have collected. The story can be about people in the news like Susan Lucci, who has finally won her Emmy; Mark McGwire, who hugged his son after his 62nd homer; or John Glenn, who went into space at age 75. It is relatively easy to discover, develop, and deliver simple stories to use as openers. The speaker can then move into the body of the speech having already connected with the audience in a positive way. A minister who addresses the same congregation week in and week out can establish a reputation as an interesting and enjoyable storyteller. Some stories will be more memorable than others, but any story is better than a solemn announcement about the deacons' meeting or the bulletin committee report.

*Open with a Question:* I recently spoke to a gathering of franchise owners of a popular fast-food chain. In my research I had found that their primary problem was finding and keeping young employees. My opening line was, "Would you like to learn more about how you can hire and keep good employees, and make them happy?"

A simple question, and one whose answer they were interested in. We were off and running. In that one question, they had been given a hint at where we were going in the program.

Would you like to be a better golfer?

Would you like to learn how to be a better parent?

What if you could make more money, work less, and have less stress?

A quick question engages the listeners instantly, whereas "It's good to be in Topeka" allows the audience to remain on hold.

*Try a Daring Surprise Opener:* Back to context for a moment. A daring spontaneous opener can be a home run, but one must be careful and certain that it will work. Within the context of a particular event, a speaker will often find an opener that is better than anything that was planned. Pay careful attention during programs by previous speakers, remarks by the emcee, awards given to attendees, or introductions of honored guests or board members.

After innumerable awards had been given, as many as 50, each with a plaque and a picture snapped, I was introduced. It was getting late and I chose this opener: "Did you hear about the guy who won the lottery today? Hey, I'd just like to be the guy that sold you all those plaques!"

The line is not original with me. I'd heard it years before and recalled it in that moment. It worked very well in that context, because the audience had become aware that almost everyone in the room had received an award. I then said, "If you can't get an award in this company, you need to attend the training class at six in the morning."

That was a bit of a risk, but the audience loved the riskiness of the comment and secretly agreed with me. Careful, though; do not offend management.

The Daring Surprise Opener can be the most effective in audience enjoyment, because it relates to the moment and the context of this unique event. The problem is that there is no guarantee that your prepared ad lib will work. If it does work, it is more powerful than a prepared story; but if it doesn't work, you may dig a hole that is tough to get out of.

It's up to the speaker to understand the context, the audience, the mood, and the time and place, and to create according to one's best intuition.

## SPONTANEOUS HUMOR

As we discussed earlier, humor and story go together like turkey and dressing. Humor is crucial to successful speaking.

Planned humor is essential and can connect with the audience in a high-impact way. But, believe it or not, spontaneous humor will almost always bring forth the loudest, longest laugh from an audience. Why? For one thing, they seem to sense that it is spontaneous. Sometimes they are wrong about that. I use several lines that seem spontaneous but are carefully planned. For example, when the ball is coming at me in my second at-bat in the Fishook story, I say, "Thank God it was lower this time, don't b'lieve I could have taken two to the head that day." This gets a good laugh, a planned laugh line. Being from Arkansas, I was always expected to have a line or two of humor about President

Clinton. So, on one occasion in the middle of his impeachment trial, I added spontaneously, "I might have ended up President!" Boom! Huge laugh. It was unexpected, even by me, and the audience sensed it. They could feel spontaneity in my tone and body energy, and we all responded with surprise and laughter.

There is no need to analyze the line for its humor, for that is almost impossible. My point is that it was spontaneous in nature. Any good line is a keeper, so I began to use it all the time. I had to be very, very careful not to let it become rote or planned. It always works, is not an insult to the president, and is considered good-natured ribbing. But I confess that no matter how hard I try to make that line truly spontaneous, it does not get the surprised explosion of laughter it received the very first time, when it was in fact a surprise even to me.

Thus, a lesson learned. Spontaneity contains a dimension of chemistry and a metaphysical quality that cannot be dissected or explained. Whenever possible, it is best to find spontaneous bits of humor in the moment.

Yes, it does require some talent. I didn't say it was easy. Humorists have a talent, a slant, and a gift for seeing life slightly askew. That's why they are humorists.

## SPEAKING OF TIME

One of my most successful speeches was one hour and forty minutes long. It was a fabulous audience and I used almost every bit of material I knew. In another context, the Million Dollar Round Table, I was held strictly to 20 minutes. That was what I had planned. In truth, 20 minutes was almost too brief a segment of time to tell the four stories they wanted me to tell and wrap up with some brief points. I spoke for 28 minutes and it was one of the best presentations of my career. From 28 minutes to 100 minutes is a long span, but both can be appropriate depending on the context.

Overall, if you can't deliver your message in 40 minutes, you are likely trying to say too much. A speaker is trying to deliver a message; not a dozen messages, not even three messages, but one message. I suggest a 40-minute speech as a maximum length even for a professional speaker. Only with much sizzle, props, video clips, pictures, or humor can a speaker sustain audience attention for much more than 40 minutes.

*Titanic,* the most popular movie ever, was more than three hours long. A Broadway play can be two hours long with intermission. A baseball game can be three hours long, but you can grab a hot dog, drink a beer, go to the john, do the wave, or go home. A TV sitcom is a half-hour and a drama is one hour long. A sermon is about 25 minutes, but feels like an eternity.

A speech? Don't push your luck. Less is more.

## CLOSING POWERFULLY

Save one of your most powerful stories, lines, or punch lines for the very end. Most of us have heard the saying about speaking, "Tell them what you're going to tell them, tell them, then tell them what you told them." Not a bad little saying.

Wrap up the speech with the point of the speech. Allow the audience to walk out with the main point in their minds, and on an emotional high from a very funny line or story. In a speech that I call "One Leg at a Time," I close the speech by telling the story of me standing on the high school football field—called Smith-Robinson Stadium—where I wanted to be a football star for my football coach father. My last line is about being on "his" field, not playing football, but making a speech at the high school commencement some 30 years later.

The symbolism is all there: the second son trying to gain his father's approval, the mother who encouraged him to just be himself, a comedian perhaps, or an artist; the adult now standing on that field. Here are my exact words: "While five thousand people laughed at my stories, I looked up and noticed the name on the stadium, Grady Robinson Stadium. And so I thought, well, here I am, standing on his field, starring in a sense, not playing football but holding a baton."

I hold the microphone in the exact position I used earlier in the speech when I hinted to my father that I would not play football but would be in the band.

"You don't play one of them instruments do you son?"

"No. Mama said I could get a baton ..."

As modern fathers and mothers think about their own children being drum majors in the band, there is a big laugh. Closure: Our hero has returned and has managed to Find the Victory. Wrap-up: A psychological close for the entire journey or cycle. But this is show biz, and we're not done yet.

"There was wonderful closure that night as I received hugs from childhood friends and family. And, yes, my old Canary reading buddy, Elmer Joe Tackett."

There is anticipatory laughter before I add, "He's doing real good—he's a White House lawyer."

If I am speaking to schoolteachers and staff and the superintendent is likable and popular, I can say, "He's a real success—he's a superintendent of schools."

Or, as was the case at the Million Dollar Round Table, I consider the context again. I used one of their most despised competitors, whom I will not mention here. I said, "Elmer Joe is a real success these days—he's an agent for _____."

The line just brought the house down. Yes, it's exaggeration and fiction, pure humor, and the audience is fully aware that I'm pulling their legs.

Be your own unique, authentic self. It's a critical but simple message for all. Close with perhaps the biggest laugh of the program and walk off to a standing ovation.

Wrap up the point of the speech with a kind of return or victory, just like the Hero's Journey motif. And leave them, if possible, on an emotional, read humorous, note.

The audience will remember most what they hear last. Stand-up comics save their best bit for the very end of the set. On *The Tonight Show* or at your local comedy club, the experienced comedian moves toward the close of the material and with confidence hits the final punch line. The anticipated audience response is received with a bow, a wave of the hand, and a "Thank you, you've been great."

Speakers would do well to learn from hardworking comedians, who have learned a bit of showbiz and know the importance of the close.

Compare the many corporate programs when the speaker says something like, "Well, that's just about all I have for now. Any questions?" There is a deathly silence in the audience. The speaker stares out at them and there is a moment of uncertainty. The speaker is wondering, "Did I answer all the questions and therefore consider my program a success?" Or, "Could it be that no one is remotely interested in the topic to begin with?" What an awful way to close a speech.

## Strong Closers

Depending on the event, make a determination whether you wish to close with humor or thoughtfulness.

If you choose humor, save one of your best stories or jokes for the close. Say "Thank you" amidst the laughter, and wave and bow with a smile.

If you choose thoughtfulness, close with a quiet and sincere tone, challenging them to go out there and implement your message, then pause, and then say, "Thank you." No wave is necessary, nor is a big smile needed. Your intent is thoughtfulness. Walk away thoughtfully, leaving the audience a moment to ponder your message before moving on to other challenges, ideas, and programming.

## Audience Feedback

After the speech, many audience members will want to talk with you to share an event, an anecdote, or an insight that your speech has evoked. An experienced speaker is aware that this moment of personal dialogue is vitally important for both speaker and audience member. Sometimes there is disagreement. The speaker should listen carefully and consider the point of disagreement with respect and, if appropriate, offer in kind fashion a defense of your stance or statement. Usually those in disagreement feel respected and the issue finds closure quickly.

Audience members often have their own versions of your story. After I tell "Facing Fishook," there is always a man or two who will share his own story. Sometimes we go deeper into the ramifications of their own reaction, self-image issues in later life, insights about competition and parents attempting to make little men out of their boys, and many other issues. This one-on-one dialogue is very important in the speaker–audience relationship. Barriers have been brought down and there is an experience of deep human contact.

Those speakers who are more interested in intellectual dissemination of information will elicit a response from the audience that is on the same level they chose to speak. The Teapot-style speaker will connect with the audience on that formal, intellectual level.

## SUMMARY

Use your own authenticity as a speaker. Take the microphone in hand and tell your story with confidence. Open with a current shared experience that you try your best to tie to that group. Or use a simple story that will immediately gain attention. Use sound and lighting wisely. Be in the flow and dare to risk spontaneous humor that relates to this place and time, this context. Be aware of time. Close powerfully with one of your best moments, and tie it back to your opening, if possible. Close by restating the point of the speech and, if at all possible, with humor.

# 17 USING THE GIFT: MASTERING PUBLIC SPEAKING

n all honesty, I suspect that successful speaking is more mystery than mastery. Most successful speakers I know personally will admit in privacy that they were given this strange gift of gab as a child. They've worked hard to develop their craft as a speaker or humorous storyteller, but in fact it seems to be God-given. The fact that I was surprisingly calm that day as I was introduced to the Million Dollar Round Table, the most expectant and demanding audience on the American platform, may say more about my own strange personality than about my ability as a speaker. Fully aware that a home run would elevate me in the speaking business and lead to dozens of speaking dates, and realizing that I was being paid the highest fee of my speaking career, it was and is surprising that I could remain calm.

It is no secret that most adults rate public speaking as one of the most dreaded and feared experiences. How was it that I could remain calm?

At that time I was in my twentieth year of storytelling and my tenth year of professional speaking. I had been in similar situations many, many times before. About to be introduced to a crowd of people who were total strangers, I was able to reflect back on my own past speaking engagements and be confident that my stories, my humor, my voice, and my life journey would connect at the deepest level with that audience.

I have come to view speaking as a unique art form. Every event that I have ever spoken at has been unique. That's why I have stated over and over in this book that correct understanding of the context with its myriad of relational dynamics is of primary importance. A misunderstanding of the context can lead to disaster. An address to a high school football team moments before the kickoff of the big game is not the time or place for 15 minutes of your most inspirational material. Adaptability may be one of the most critical success factors for a speaker.

The minute you assume that you have a situation well in hand and that your program will be a smash hit, the context shifts slightly and you are received with polite applause or a stifled yawn. Recently in Sacramento I looked over the audience and the context and feared that I would not go over well in that particular situation. To my surprise, they were warm and enthusiastic. You never really know for sure.

I understand speaking to be transrational; it is above or beyond mere rational analysis or explanation. The secrets of effective speaking lie just beyond the door of reason. It is an unexplainable and perhaps unteachable mixture of a host of human factors. And yet, we continue to try to dissect it, analyze it, explain it, and teach it. We do that by dissecting the separate parts. But the essence is in the mixing of the parts.

There is something mysterious about the mix of separate parts. The secret is in the mixing, or the relationship of the many separate parts.

## What Speaking Is Not

1. Speaking is not acting, although there are moments when we act. The actor traditionally utters the words of another person, the scriptwriter. The speaker speaks from the heart, his or her own words flowing out of conviction. Acting in the proper place can win you an Oscar, but a speaker who is accused of acting is considered a phony.

2. Speaking is not a performance, but we perform certain segments of material. I much prefer the word *presence* to *performance* when referring to speaking. The Latin term "per" means through. We look through to a "form," hinting of a hidden barrier between performer and audience. Speakers are in "presence" rather than performing. We are one with the audience.

3. Speaking is not stand-up comedy, although humor is one of the critical success factors in speaking. Stand-up comedy, a powerful art form in itself, is designed for pure entertainment (although powerful lessons and insights are available) and success is measured in LPMs (Laughs Per Minute). A speaker uses humor wisely, weaving in personal stories, jokes, puns, and ad libs that are funny but also carrying a clear message. There is a point to the story and the speaker is free to offer proper commentary.

4. Speaking is not teaching, but the speaker often teaches. The teacher imparts information; the speaker does also, but with the power of persuasion. Training, education, and teaching may occur in a variety of settings. Speaking is not always a part of teaching or education.

5. Speaking is not just storytelling, though it's rather obvious I am an advocate of the power of personal story. The speaker uses the power of story to make a point and in a conscious attempt to sell that point.

Speaking is a unique process combining information (reasoned thinking) and inspiration (story, symbol, humor) to move listeners to a desired place of perceiving, thinking, or "seeing."

## A SECRET BEYOND THE PHYSICAL COMPONENTS

By physical components I mean the obvious tools of human communication—the unique larynx and jaw hinges of the human species. We are the only species capable of talking the way we do. Recent research reveals communication sounds in many animals such as whales, porpoises, and gorillas, but nothing as complex as the human tongue, breath, and brain memory of sounds that make our language system work.

The eyes, face, hands, and body movements make up the very important visual aspect of the speaker. We now know that body movement and visual signals play a huge role in communication. In public speaking, sight and sound are the dominant domains, as opposed to touch or smell.

There are also qualities beyond the physical, which I call, for lack of a better term, metaphysical qualities. One of these is humor. But, how do you analyze humor? You don't.

Or consider stage presence. How does one person walk out on a stage and command attention, when another person walks out and people are immediately disinterested or even irritated? How does that happen? These are qualities that we can only call metaphysical, because they are beyond rational explanation.

Meta qualities are presence, the message, enthusiasm, compassion, sincerity, and authenticity, to name a few. We see and hear the results of enthusiasm in the voice tension and excited body language of the speaker, but we do not actually see enthusiasm. We see physical manifestation of metaphysical realities.

We hear sincerity in voice tones and rhythms, and see sincerity in certain facial expressions of the speaker. The physical elements of facial expression and a metaphysical element like sincerity blend together and give birth to such unique artistic characteristics as voice intonations, rhythms, phrasing, pauses, and gestures—an authentic combination that can produce individual genius.

Frank Sinatra is recognized as rare genius who used intonation, pronunciation of words, and phrasing to a level of artistry. How did he do that? Not being a musical expert, the genius of Sinatra is beyond me. The same can be said of Louie Armstrong. He is considered by many critics to be the premier musical genius of American history. Louie had a very gravelly voice, pronounced words in a rather strange way, did not read music in the classic style, and yet all summed up to pure genius.

How did his unique combination of elements make Will Rogers the most beloved man in America? Will Rogers was a speaker and commentator, yet he too is a deep mystery to me. Will stammered, yammered, scratched his head, chewed gum, and constantly repeated himself. He would not receive a passing evaluation from the local Toastmaster's club due to his "ya knows" and "uh-huhs," and yet to this day he is considered one of America's most beloved speechmakers. How does that happen?

I'm convinced that soul leads speakers to pronounce words with a slightly personal intonation and phrasing. The unique genius of Rogers, Armstrong, and Sinatra is just that: a unique combination of separate components.

Speaking is relational and context-dependent—like golf. Speaking can be compared to a golf swing. Even the best players on the PGA tour have unique swings. Teaching experts can dissect and quickly analyze the many separate components of the very best golf swings, only to discover that all "perfect" swings are discernibly different. We then realize that it is not the separate component parts that make a successful swing, but rather how the parts relate to each other. A speaker who uses story and humor may have all the separate component parts seemingly in perfect order, only to discover that they don't work well in relationship to each other.

You can have all the right elements, but often the key is how they relate to each other at a particular point in time and space. The common denominator in golf is balance. We search for the key secret ingredient of speaking. It is to the speaker what balance is to the golfer. But what is that secret ingredient?

## THE MYSTERY OF THE RELATIONSHIPS

All metaphysical qualities are not of equal value. It is in this area that we dare to attempt to know the unknowable, to look behind the veil, to peel the layers of the onion and look inside genius or charisma. A speaker can have enthusiasm, a very important metaphysical quality, and have no true compassion, but if a speaker has true compassion, we assume she also has enthusiasm.

A speaker can have enthusiasm, which I have already stated is one of the most important aspects of speaking. But if the speaker is enthusiastic about making money, selling a lot of widgets, and becoming wealthy, which could be devoid of community concerns, love of neighbor, and concern about the environment, that enthusiasm loses some value.

A speaker can be totally sincere about his message and be totally wrong; consider Jim Jones or David Koresh.

When I attempted to determine a hierarchy of values, I ran into all kinds of roadblocks. I worked my way to the deepest or highest metaphysical quality, the quality that would include all the others, and finally (after weeks of thinking about enthusiastic but humorless speaking, humorous but angry speaking, compassionate but illogical speaking, enthusiastic but dead-wrong speaking) arrived at sincerity.

It seemed for a while that I'd found it. The sincere speaker must possess all the qualities mentioned. Then, speaking coach and friend Max Dixon casually destroyed my whole theory when he said, "You can be a sincere speaker and be utterly boring."

Well, yes.

The speaker must not mechanically dish out information. The speaker combines the human factor, the soul factor, and the Divine factor through the use of story art to connect at a higher or deeper level.

The body and its parts become instruments of art when the metaphysical qualities are "seen" through eyes and "heard" through ears not just as sensory empirical observations but as something transcending, through voice intonation, word pronunciation, rhythms of words and sounds, and the use of silence. Flaming, passionate eyes reflect passion from life's true experiences lived and processed and accepted, not rejected. Hands and arms somehow, with a wave and a twist, communicate meta-meanings arising out of the highest meta-qualities. Body placement becomes congruent with the fire of the message, with body language so subtle as to be beyond explanation, born and developed in our ancestors at a protoplasmic stage long before the voice box was developed.

I've heard thousands of speakers over the past 25 years in every conceivable setting—from church pulpits to the Million Dollar Round Table to hotel meeting rooms. Those I recall as soul-impact speakers contained a common trait, a quality or value that lifted them above the pack. There was passion of message and therefore enthusiasm, well-developed stories delivered with humor and timing, a viewpoint that moved or persuaded sincerely to seeing things anew. This common denominator that is to the speaker what balance is to the golfer is a quality underlying all. I believe now it is given birth and nurtured in a pure, authentic life story, the secret ingredient is your authentic journey.

To me the authentic story of every human being is pure genius. The hero who has journeyed into the forest where no other trail was seen is living an authentic once-in-a-universe story. Those who hold back, who fear to journey and therefore rely on information passed down from others about what lies beyond, are merely copy cats and have no authentic story to tell.

My story is not the greatest story of all time. My story is certainly not the most successful one according to societal measures of fame, power, and money. My story has not been the most adventurous or the best-thought-out journey. And I have not always fought with courage or made the proper decisions at the proper time. But it is my journey, my story, my once-in-a-universe adventure. It is authentic.

So, that day, in one of the important milestones of my life journey, I approached the microphone, smiled at 4,000 strangers, and said, "Did I ever tell y'all about the time my daddy decided I should be a football player ...?"

# POSTSCRIPT

I am always a little shocked when an audience member, after listening to a series of my stories about growing up in Arkansas, feels the need to ask such questions as, "Grady Jim, are you really from Arkansas?" or "Grady, are those stories true?"

The storyteller is an artist, not a science teacher, math teacher, preacher, or news anchor. The storyteller is a yarn spinner, a jokester, and a trickster—a modern mythmaker. I have chosen to spin my stories around true characters: my father, mother, brother, and sister. Those characters are real, but they are obviously romanticized, embellished, exaggerated, and memorialized.

"Yes, my father was a coach. My mother was a teacher. My brother was perfect and my little sister was six years younger."

"So, where are they now?"

"My sister is the mother of three, recently a grandmother, a successful businesswoman and avid tennis player in Fort Smith, Arkansas. My brother, David, is in his 34th year at Sheridan Schools and is now superintendent, father of two grown children, and, uncharacteristically for Dave, host of his own weekly radio show playing rowdy, rousing zydeco-cajun music."

"Your father?"

"In 1977, only weeks after my mother's death as a result of cancer, I was standing beside my car in the driveway of our home at 701 N. Main in Greenwood, Arkansas. Daddy leaned on my car door, saying nothing. He had been deeply saddened by the death of my mother and seemed reluctant to let me leave for my home in Memphis. I said, "Dad, are you okay?" He nodded but didn't speak. Something was bothering him. I got out of the car and stood beside him. He looked down to the ground. There was a tear in his eye. "Dad," I mumbled. Never having said the "L" word out loud, I stammered, "I want you to know I love you." He didn't look up. I didn't expect a response. I knew. He knew. Then suddenly he looked up, teary-eyed but clear-voiced, and said, "I love you too, son." I drove to Memphis with those words dancing in my heart. That night, he died.

\* \* \*

These days I live in Lovell, Arkansas, not far from the University of Arkansas where I intend to pursue a masters degree in Fine Arts in Creative Writing. On a nice summer day, I was strolling across campus reminiscing about the past, reading the names of famous old Razorback football players on the senior walk. I walked with head down, reading the names of the senior class of 1969. Suddenly finding the R's, a feeling of presence came over me a split second before I saw her name. Wilma Robinson. Thirty-five years after her two years at Central Baptist College in Conway (1934–35), my mother received her bachelor's degree from the University of Arkansas. Twenty-two years after her death, I stood over her name on the Senior Walk of 1969. I am an emotional guy. I admit it. My mother supported me, recognized the real me, and encouraged my humor and creative nature. She was the chief influence of my childhood and therefore my whole life. I bent down and gently ran my fingers across each letter of her name, attempting to reach out and touch her as she had reached out as a loving mother to touch me.

The human story is life-giving, uplifting, tender, inspiring, and funny, filled with wonder and awe. It is deeply painful at times, challenging, requiring courage, faith, and hope. Your story is life-shaping, inspiring, hilarious, and it is *your* story. Tell it.

# REFERENCES

Boorstein, D. *The Seekers: The Story of Man's Continuing Quest to Understand His World.* Vintage Books, 1998.

Busby, M. *Larry McMurtry and the West: An Ambivalent Relationship.* Texas Writers Series, University of North Texas Press, 1995.

Campbell, J. *Hero with a Thousand Faces.* Bollengen Series, Princeton University Press, 1949.

————. *The Power of Myth.* Doubleday, New York, 1989.

————. In *Mythic Worlds, Modern Words: On the Art of James Joyce.* E. Epstein, ed. HarperCollins, New York, 1993.

Erickson, M. and E. Rossi. *Hypnotherapy: An Explanatory Casebook.* Irvington Publishers.

Ferguson, M. *The Aquarian Conspiracy.* J. P. Tarcher, 1980.

Jung, C. G. *The Portable Jung.* Edited by Joseph Campbell. Penguin Books, 1971.

McAdams, D. *Stories We Live By.* Guilford Press, 1993.

Reynolds, D. *Walt Whitman's America.* Vintage Books, 1996.

Small, J. *Transformers: The Artist of Self Creation.* Devorss Publications, 1982.

Tarnas, R. *The Passion of the Western Mind.* Harmony Books, 1991.

# REFERENCES

Torrance, R. *The Spiritual Quest: Transcendence in Myth, Religion, and Science.* University of California Press, 1994.

Vogler, C. *The Writer's Journey: Mythic Structure for Storytellers and Screenwriters.* Michael Wise Productions Book, 1992.

Wilber, K. *Sex, Ecology, Spirituality.* Shambhala Press, 1993.

# INDEX

# INDEX

# INDEX

# INDEX